Our Own Stories

Cross-Cultural Communication Practice

Our Own Stories

Cross-Cultural Communication Practice

Norine Dresser

Longman

Our Own Stories: Cross-Cultural Communication Practice

Longman, 10 Bank Street, White Plains, N. Y. 10606

Associated companies:
Longman Group Ltd., London
Longman Cheshire Pty., Melbourne
Longman Paul Pty., Auckland
Copp Clark Pitman, Toronto

Distributed in the United Kingdom by Longman Group Ltd.,
Longman House, Burnt Mill, Harlow, Essex, CM20 2JE,
England and by associated companies, branches, and
representatives throughout the world.

Acquisitions director: Joanne Dresner
Senior development editor: Debbie Sistino
Development editor: Randee Falk
Production editor: Janice L. Baillie
Text design: Jack Schwartz
Cover design: Joseph DePinho
Cover photo: Provided by Guidance Associates
Text art: Karen Henrickson Sothoron
Production supervisor: Richard Bretan

Library of Congress Cataloging-in-Publication Data
Our own stories: cross-cultural communication practice/
  [compiled by] Norine Dresser.
        p.   cm.
    ISBN 0-8013-0983-2
      1. English language—Textbooks for foreign speakers.
    2. Intercultural communication—Problems, exercises, etc. 3. United
    States—Civilization—Problems, exercises, etc. 4. College prose,
    American—California—Los Angeles. 5. Culture—Problems, exercises,
    etc. 6. American essays—Minority authors. 7. Readers—United
    States. I. Dresser, Norine.
    PE1128.O97 1993
    428.6'4—dc20   92-33241
                                                          CIP

3 4 5 6 7 8 9-CRS-98 97 96 95 94

DEDICATION

In loving memory of my father, Issidore Shapiro,
who understood the power of a tale well told.

CONTENTS

INTRODUCTION

Our Own Stories is based upon cross-cultural communication misunderstandings described in essays written by students at California State University, Los Angeles. Most of these students were born in Asia and Latin America, yet regardless of their origin their stories are universal—the theme of the outsider trying to become part of a new culture. The students wrote about their astounding experiences in response to the following assignment: "Describe a time when cultural differences caused a problem for you in this country." The resulting essays—sad, funny, and inspiring—are the backbone of this book and the centerpiece of each unit. Written from the heart, they demonstrate that the road to becoming a new American is filled with many bumps and wrong turns. Therefore, these stories give encouragement to other ESL students by showing that every newcomer makes mistakes. In addition, the tales point to the problem areas in understanding American culture, which usually center around customs, beliefs, and/or values. Further, the stories reveal that it is advantageous to be familiar with the customs of the many different groups of people who live here.

Our Own Stories is designed for intermediate ESL students to improve their conversation and reading skills as well as provide information about American culture. There are twenty units and each one begins with a real student's dilemma caused by cultural differences. Each unit deals with one particular custom—for example, food taboos. Although it is not mandatory that the units be followed in sequence, please note that the earlier part of the book deals with simpler cultural issues, while those essays toward the back relate to more complex and sophisticated subjects.

Within each unit are diversified activities to develop discussion about the topic and to build English-language skills through exercises such as comprehension and inference questions, vocabulary development, role plays, interviews, and oral and written reports.

Activities have been designed to be as self-explanatory as possible and flexibility has been allowed for. For example, teachers may select one unit and use it over more than one class meeting, or if there are time limitations, they may skip some of the later activities within the unit—for instance, Role Play or Follow-Up. However, to get the maximum from each unit, it is recommended that all sections (described below) be used.

Do you know...

The questions and accompanying illustration in this section are designed to focus the students' attention on the topic and to anticipate where the cultural conflict might lie. Through discussion, teachers and students become aware of what they already know about the particular cultural issue.

The Story

Reading the story twice is a good way to ensure understanding. One method is to have students first read to themselves. The second time they can take turns reading aloud one line at a time. In this way it becomes apparent where students are having problems with pronunciation. If they stumble, this may also be a signal that they are unfamiliar with the vocabulary. Anticipated new words with their definitions appear on the page.

Comprehension

Three sets of questions follow each story. The first two focus on comprehension. Section A requires true/false responses while Section B adds a little more complexity by asking students to give answers in phrases or sentences. Section C asks for students' opinions. This is important training because in some parts of the world, student opinions are never asked for. However, since having an opinion and drawing inferences are valued in American education, it is important that students get practice in this skill, particularly if they plan to go on to higher education.

CULTURE CAPSULE

This section contains information about American cultural rules. Students can read to themselves or to each other, or if preferred, the teacher may want to read aloud to the class and then ask questions to ensure comprehension.

Cultural Exchange

This activity focuses on similarities and differences in cultures. Having students describe their own cultural customs fosters pride in their own heritage. At the same time, they are learning about their classmates' backgrounds, which may be similar to or distinct from their own. This presents a perfect opportunity for helping students develop respect for one another's culture. One way to do this is by avoiding judgmental words like "strange" or "weird," which some students might want to use in evaluating their classmates' traditions. Teachers might point out that it is difficult to be objective about another culture without complete information about the values and customs of that culture.

Expansion

The focus of Expansion is on the rules and customs of American culture through activities that improve vocabulary skills. Students may be asked to complete a crossword puzzle or a word search, conduct a survey, or participate in decision-making activities. Answers to the puzzles appear at the back of the book.

Role Play

There are two role-play situations in each unit. Generally the first one re-enacts the story in the unit while the second one presents a parallel situation. Before acting, students develop a script. Guided questions are provided to lead students in considering motivation for the characters' actions and words.

Role play encourages students to have fun while improvising with the language. In addition, students may work out some of their own cultural conflicts when pretending to be other non-English speakers. On the other hand, when portraying Americans, they can try on another perspective to see how it feels to be in a position of authority.

Follow-Up

The first activity requires students to prepare either a written or oral report. Not only does this bring closure to the unit, but it also sharpens skills that will move the student toward the next level of language proficiency.

The second follow-up can be done in class, time permitting, or can be used as an extra-credit, take-home assignment. These activities are quite varied throughout the book.

Finally, I would like to know how ESL classes enjoy this book. If teachers or students have any suggestions or comments, I would be pleased to hear from them. If teachers use the same writing assignment that was the basis of *Our Own Stories* ("Describe a time when cultural differences caused a problem for you in this country."), and they have responses they would like to share, or if students would like to send me their own responses to this topic, I would appreciate receiving them. Please write to me at the following address:

Norine Dresser
c/o Longman Publishing Group
ESL Editorial Department
10 Bank Street
White Plains, NY 10606-1951

ACKNOWLEDGMENTS

Every book begins as an Aha!, and the inspiration for *Our Own Stories* occurred when I read sixty student essays on the topic of cultural differences. Charmed, I discussed the possibilities of collecting more examples to create a book and received excellent feedback and assistance from my colleagues at California State University, Los Angeles, and those who teach elsewhere. I am grateful to all of them: Nancy Allison, David Beaulieu, Lise Buranen, Mike Cappella, Rosella Cappella, Virginia Crane, Chloe Diepenbrock, Sally Gardner (and her great ACLP teachers), Karen Gregg, Bill Hart, Jayasri Hart, Nancy Hutcheon, Elliott Oring, Michael Pessah, Morris Polan, Buddy Roberts, Arpi Sarafian, Sharon Smartt, and Nick Zonen.

In addition, I was indeed fortunate to have met Joanne Dresner, Director of ESL Acquisitions and Development at Longman Publishing Group, who immediately recognized the possibilities in my embryonic idea, gave me encouragement, and eventually—the green light. I toast her vision and all her kindness. Further, I would like to express appreciation to Debbie Sistino, Senior Development Editor, who worked closely with me. Her guidance was always sensitive, clear-cut, and reassuring. I also thank Randee "Hawkeye" Falk for all her "right-on" suggestions and fine-tuned editing.

To my consortium of gifted friends upon whom I selfishly rely for consultation on all projects—Kay Enell, Montserrat Fontes, Janice Garey, and Jan Steward—I say, "Thanks, buddies, I couldn't have done it without your help!"

Of course, this book could never have come to fruition without the support of my husband, Harold, who endured my complaints and grouchiness, yet lovingly made rush trips to the post office and stationery supply store and brought in all those great take-out dinners.

Finally, one of my fondest memories is when, as an elementary-school girl, I helped my two European-born grandmothers with writing assignments from their adult-school English classes. I relished the position of child being teacher to grown-ups. Today, as a grandmother myself, I still feel the same pleasure, this time in helping young students learn English. Thus, it is to the memory of my first students, grandmothers Anna Friesh and Ida Shapiro, and my wonderful CSULA composition students that this book is dedicated. I pay tribute to the hundreds who shared their delightful stories with me and, in particular, those student authors whose adventures were selected for inclusion here. I offer you my heartfelt gratitude.

Student Authors

Juan Carlos Cardenas	Chau Phu
Norma Garcia	Rosa A. Rodriguez-Cabral
John C. Gomez, Jr.	Kin Tchang
Janice Nghi Nha Ha	Hoa T. Van
Raymond Kwong	Norma A. Velasco
Tuan Lam	Yung Ho Wang
Yuxue Li	Pat Wong
Le My Lien	Lynn Cheng-Ping Yang
Monica Martinez	Tony Yang
Chieng Pe	Catherine Yee

Our Own Stories

Cross-Cultural Communication Practice

UNIT 1
Clothing

? Do you know...

1. What do most Americans wear to school?
2. What do teachers wear?

The Dress of Lace

Read the story.

My name is Linh. I'm an eighteen-year-old girl. My ethnic background and native language are Vietnamese. This is a story about what happened to me on my first day of school in America. I was nine years old.

A few weeks before school started, my aunt, my uncle, and some of my dad's friends came to visit us and they brought a lot of presents. I was surprised when I found clothing in one of the boxes. The clothes were nice but ordinary. They weren't special or fancy except for one dress. It was a dress of lace. There was lace surrounding the neck and the sleeves and lace on the bottom. I was very happy when I saw this dress.

On the first day of school I wanted to look my best and impress the other students. I wanted them to make friends with me, so I put on my fancy dress of lace. But when I got to school, all the students stared at me. They were laughing and saying something in English. I didn't know why they were doing this. I thought that maybe they had never seen an Asian girl in a dress before or that they wanted to make friends with me but were embarrassed to come over.

In the classroom an American teacher spoke English to me and pointed at my dress, but I didn't know what she was saying so I just smiled. The whole morning she didn't let me walk around or stand up. I had to sit all the way in the last row in the back of the room. During lunch when all the other students had gone, an Asian teacher came into the room. The minute she saw me she spoke to me in Vietnamese. She told me that I shouldn't wear a nightgown to school, that in America people only wear nightgowns to sleep in! I was so embarrassed that I almost burst into tears. That morning when I left home, I thought I looked good, but I didn't. Instead, I embarrassed myself on my first day of school. I felt like not going to school anymore.

This embarrassment taught me not to try to impress others or I might end up making a fool out of myself. I also learned the difference between a fancy dress and a nightgown!

ethnic—Cultural, religious, national, or racial group

lace—A cloth that is made of fine threads and looks like net

nightgown—A piece of woman's clothing, like a loose dress to sleep in

fool—A person who acts unwisely

Comprehension

A. *Tell whether these sentences are true or false.*

1. Linh came to the United States when she was eighteen years old.

2. Linh and her parents have other relatives in the United States.

3. Linh wore her dress of lace in a store.

4. Linh wore her dress of lace on the first day of school.

5. Linh's schoolmates were surprised when they saw her because they had never seen an Asian girl in a dress before.

6. The American teacher put Linh in the back of the classroom.

7. As soon as the American teacher explained the problem, Linh understood.

8. Linh did not enjoy her first day of school.

B. *Answer these questions.*

1. How did Linh get her dress of lace?

2. Why did Linh want to wear the dress of lace to school?

3. What did Linh's schoolmates do when they saw her?

4. What did the American teacher have Linh do? Why?

5. When did Linh find out she was wearing a nightgown?

6. How did Linh feel when she found out she was wearing a nightgown?

C. *Give your opinion.*

1. Do you think Linh's classmates behaved badly toward her?

2. What do you think Linh's teacher should have done?

3. Linh says she learned that she should not try to impress others. Do you agree with Linh's conclusion? Why or why not?

4. What kind of clothes would you wear on your first day of school or work? Explain your choice.

5. Suppose you were going someplace and you did not know what would be appropriate to wear. What would you do?

CULTURE CAPSULE

Students usually wear casual, not formal, clothes to school. Jeans, T-shirts, and sneakers are popular among both girls and boys. It is also acceptable to dress up more. Students dress according to their personal preferences and sometimes are influenced by fads, or the latest fashions.

In some private schools and religious schools, students wear uniforms. Although public schools do not use uniforms, they sometimes have "dress codes," or rules about what clothes may *not* be worn to school.

fads—Short-lived popular interests or practices

Cultural Exchange

A. *Fill in the chart below and then share your answers with your classmates. Look at the following places. For each place, write down what clothes you would wear in your country and what clothes people wear in the United States.*

What Do People Wear . . .	Your Country	United States
To school?		
To work?		
To the supermarket?		
To a restaurant?		
To the movies?		
At home, to sleep?		

B. *Discuss these questions with your classmates.*

1. What clothing would you wear indoors in your country, but never outside in public?

2. Is there any clothing from your country that you will not wear in public in the United States?

3. Is there any American clothing you will not wear because you do not like it or because it is against the clothing customs of your culture?

4. In what ways are American clothing customs similar to clothing customs in your country? In what ways are they different?

5. What American clothing customs do you especially like?

6. Have any American clothing customs surprised you? Which ones?

Expansion

To increase your vocabulary about clothing, solve this crossword puzzle with words from the list below.

bikini	necktie	shoes	sweatsuit
bracelets	nightgown	sneakers	tuxedo
hat	purses	suit	
jacket	sandals	sunglasses	

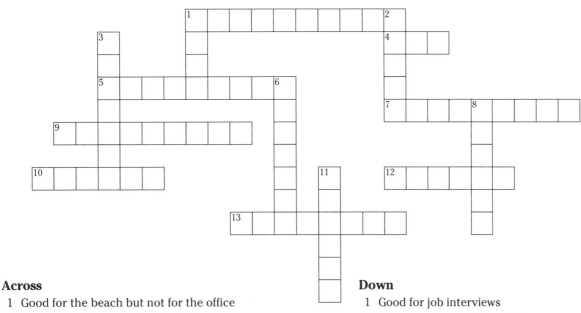

Across

1 Good for the beach but not for the office
4 Good for outdoors but not for indoors
5 Good for sleeping but not for school
7 Good for exercising but not for a wedding
9 A person can wear many of these at the same time
10 Most women carry these and some wear them on belts around their waists
12 Good for the winter but not for the summer
13 Good for the gym but not for church

Down

1 Good for job interviews
2 Some people wear them indoors; others take them off
3 Good for the summer but not for the winter
6 Good for a business meeting but not necessary for school
8 Good for a wedding but not for work
11 Good for the beach but not to go shopping

tuxedo—A man's formal evening suit, usually black

Role Play

Work in groups. Choose one of the following situations and role-play it for your classmates. Before you role-play, write the conversation.

Situation 1: Role-play "The Dress of Lace" on page 2. Begin your role play when Linh walks into school in her nightgown. What do you think happens after Linh finds out she is wearing a nightgown?

Use these questions to help you write the conversation:

☐ What do the students say to Linh? Are they mean to her?

☐ How does the American teacher try to explain the situation to Linh?

☐ Is the Asian teacher kind to Linh or does she scold her?

☐ Does Linh feel grateful when the Asian teacher explains things to her? Or is she embarrassed?

> Student A=Linh
> Student B=the American teacher
> Student C=the Asian teacher
> Students D and E=students in the school

After you role-play, discuss these questions with your classmates:

☐ How do you think Linh felt when she went to school the next day?

☐ Did you like the ending that was added?

☐ What other endings can you think of?

Situation 2: A supervisor in an office is waiting for two new employees who will start work today. The supervisor will explain their jobs to them. The new employees arrive and introduce themselves. As they do, the supervisor notices that both of them are dressed inappropriately. One worker is dressed much too formally—in a way that is good for a wedding but not for the office. The other is dressed much too informally—in a way that is good for the beach but not for the office. The supervisor must explain to them that they are dressed inappropriately.

Use these questions to help you write the conversation:

☐ How does the supervisor tell the workers they are dressed inappropriately?

☐ Do they have the same reactions or different reactions?

☐ Are they angry? Do they apologize? Do they think the supervisor is right?

> Student A=the supervisor
> Student B=the new employee who is dressed too formally
> Student C=the new employee who is dressed too informally

After you role-play, discuss these questions with your classmates:

☐ Did the supervisor convince the new employees that they were dressed inappropriately? How?

☐ What kinds of clothes do you think the two new employees will wear to work tomorrow?

☐ Do you think the new employees will be good workers? Why or why not?

Follow-Up

A. *Give a brief oral or written report. Choose number 1 or 2.*

1. Tell about a special occasion when you were either underdressed or overdressed.

2. Tell about a time when you tried to impress someone by your appearance but it did not work out as expected.

When you describe the event, consider including some of the following details:

When did this happen? Where did it take place?

Why did the event occur?

What happened? What went wrong?

How did you feel? How did others feel?

What did you learn from this experience?

B. *A friend from your native country is planning a two-week visit to the United States. He or she can bring only one suitcase. In a letter, tell your friend what clothing he or she* should *and* should not *pack.*

U N I T 2
Holidays

? Do you know...

1. How do children celebrate Halloween?
2. What are three other American holidays?

Trick or Treat?

Read the story.

Hi. My name is Tony, and I remember the first Halloween I spent in the United States. I was in the sixth grade, trying my best to study as hard as I could to overcome the language barrier. Even though I studied English in my native country, Hong Kong, I was still not able to communicate in English. I realized that my classmates were talking about how they would dress on Halloween, but I didn't know what Halloween was.

That year Halloween came on Saturday. I was home most of the day studying. I didn't have a chance to go outside and see how everyone was dressed, because if I had, the following incident would not have happened.

After dinner, my parents turned off all the lights and went to their room. They did this so they could ignore the children coming to the house for treats. But they didn't tell me about it. I was in my room, so I didn't know what was happening. After a while I went out of my room to get a drink of water. I realized that the house was dark very early, and I thought that my parents were tired after a long day of work. I didn't have any brother or sisters to come with me, so I felt very much alone in the dark house. I was not used to that. Then it happened. When I was drinking my glass of water, the doorbell rang. I looked out my window. There, standing at my front door, were four or five ghosts accompanied by a witch!

I was so scared that I started screaming and I covered myself with my blanket. I tried not to scream, but I couldn't stop. My father came running into my room asking me what was the matter. I told him about the ghosts and the witch, and he explained to me about Halloween. I was relieved after realizing the truth but I also felt embarrassed about being afraid.

That was my first experience with Halloween. Now, each year I remind my parents, weeks before Halloween, to buy candy, and when I do, my dad laughs at me about that incident.

barrier—Something that prevents progress
ignore—To take no notice of, to disregard

Comprehension

A. *Tell whether these sentences are true or false.*

1. At school Tony did not understand Halloween.

2. That year Halloween took place on a school day.

3. On Halloween, children wear their regular school clothes.

4. Tony had brothers and sisters living with him.

5. On Halloween night Tony was home alone.

6. At first Tony thought there were real ghosts and a real witch at his door.

7. Tony's parents did not understand American Halloween customs.

8. Now Tony reminds his parents to have treats ready for Halloween.

B. *Answer these questions.*

1. On Halloween day why didn't Tony notice people in their costumes?

2. On Halloween night why were the lights turned off in Tony's house?

3. Why did Tony leave his bedroom?

4. What did Tony see and do when he looked out the window?

5. How did Tony feel after his father told him about Halloween?

C. *Give your opinion.*

1. Why do you think Tony's parents didn't want the children to come to their house?

2. Why do you think the parents didn't explain the holiday to their son?

3. Why do you think Tony didn't want to scream, even though he was frightened?

4. How do you think Tony's father felt when he saw his son was so frightened?

5. Do you think Tony should be angry with his parents for not telling him about Halloween? Why or why not?

CULTURE CAPSULE

On Halloween, which comes on October 31, children go "trick or treating." The children dress up in costumes, often pretending to be something scary, like ghosts and witches. They then go from house to house asking for candy or other treats. If they do not receive any, they might threaten to play tricks—like overturning trash cans or spraying windows with shaving cream. But most children do not really play tricks.

At Halloween time, you will see many jack-o'-lanterns. These are pumpkins that have been cut to look like human faces and often have a candle inside.

Cultural  Exchange

A. *Fill in the chart below and then share your answers with your classmates. Look at the following events. For each event, write down the name of a holiday in your country and in the United States, the date when people celebrate, and one activity that takes place.*

Do People Celebrate . . .	Your Country	United States
The beginning of the new year?		
The beginning of a new season (spring, summer, fall, or winter)?		
An important religious event?		
An important historic event?		
Mother's Day, Father's Day, Grandparents' Day?		

B. *Discuss these questions with your classmates.*

1. What American holiday custom do you most enjoy?

2. What holiday custom have you learned that is from a different culture (not your culture or American culture)?

3. What holiday custom from your own culture have you introduced to an American or a person from another culture?

4. How do you celebrate birthdays?

5. For which holidays do you send greeting cards? To people from your own culture? To Americans?

Expansion

Draw a line from the name of the holiday listed in the left-hand column to the appropriate description in the right-hand column.

Christmas   Day to wear green; especially important for the Irish

New Year's Eve   Baby rabbits, colored eggs, family dinners, new clothes

Thanksgiving   Exchange gifts; fat old man with long white beard and red suit

Saint Patrick's Day   Day to honor soldiers killed in battle; parades and visits to cemeteries

April Fools' Day   Children in costume go door to door asking for treats

Easter   People play harmless tricks on one another

Halloween   Loud noises at midnight; parties, dancing

Memorial Day   Day for love and for lovers; people give cards, candies, and flowers to those they love

Fourth of July   Family gatherings, turkey dinners; Pilgrims and Indians long ago

Valentine's Day   Fireworks; picnics and barbecues

 *Role Play*

Work in pairs. Choose one of the following situations and role-play it for your classmates. Before you role-play, write the conversation.

Situation 1: Role-play "Trick or Treat?" on page 9. Begin your role play when Tony goes to get a glass of water. The doorbell rings and . . .

Use these questions to help you write the conversation:

☐ How does Tony react when he sees what is standing at his door?

☐ What does Tony's father say when he hears Tony scream?

☐ Does Tony feel embarrassed when his father explains Halloween to him or is he angry that his parents did not tell him about it earlier? Is Tony happy or relieved that there are no ghosts outside?

☐ Is Tony's father annoyed at himself for not telling Tony about Halloween, annoyed at Tony for being so afraid, or does he just want to make Tony feel better?

Student A=Tony
Student B=Tony's father

After you role-play, discuss these questions with your classmates:

☐ How did Tony feel? Was he embarrassed, angry, or relieved?

☐ How did Tony's father feel?

☐ Do you think Tony or his father could have acted some other way?

Situation 2: Two friends are at school on April 1, April Fools' Day. As an April Fools' joke, one friend tells the other that the police have just put a parking ticket on his or her car. The other friend, forgetting that it is April 1, gets very upset. Finally, the friend who played the joke says, "April fool!"

Use these questions to help you write the conversation:

☐ What does the friend say when he or she thinks there is a parking ticket on the car?

☐ When the friend says "April fool!" does the friend who has been tricked get angry or laugh at the joke?

☐ After the trick does the friend who played the trick apologize or laugh?

Student A=the friend who plays the trick about the parking ticket
Student B=the one who gets fooled

Continued on the following page

After you role-play, discuss these questions with your classmates:

☐ How did the friend feel when he or she found out the parking ticket was just an April Fools' joke?

☐ How did the friend who played the trick feel?

☐ Would you play a trick like this on April Fools' Day? Why or why not?

☐ How would you feel if someone played an April Fools' Day trick like this on you?

Follow-Up

A. *Give a brief oral or written report. Tell about a holiday that you celebrate and enjoy. When you describe the holiday, consider including some of the following details:*

What is the name of the holiday?

When does it take place?

What is the reason for this holiday? (religious? seasonal? historic? etc.)

What are some of the activities that people do on this holiday?

B. *Choose one of the celebration categories below and think of a holiday from your country that belongs to that category.*

| New Year | spring | harvest |
| winter | historic | religious |

1. Now play five-card draw. Take five 3 × 5 index cards and draw pictures that give information about the holiday. On each card you will show certain information. If you have no information about one of the categories, leave out that card.

   Information

   Card 1: What is the name of the celebration? When is it observed? What is it about?

   Card 2: Show what activities (games, rituals, etc.) there are.

   Card 3: Show what foods are prepared and eaten.

   Card 4: Show what clothing is worn.

   Card 5: Show who the participants are.

   Even if you are not a good artist, make each card as exciting as possible. Use markers, crayons, colored pens, or paste on pictures cut from magazines.

2. After you have completed the five cards, put them up on a large wall or board under the appropriate celebration heading. Compare your cards with your classmates' cards.

UNIT 3

Health and Illness

Do you know...

1. What kinds of medicines do you take if you get sick with a cold or the flu?

2. Do you know anyone who has been healed by someone who was not a doctor or a nurse?

Coining

Read the story.

My father was born in China, and my mother was born in Cambodia. They adopted the traditional values of their cultures and passed these values on to me. I was also born in Cambodia, but my family and I have been living in the United States for about ten years now. I have even chosen an American name and call myself Wendy.

There were not many Asian students where I first went to school, so when I got sick I didn't know what to do, whether to stay home or go to school. One day when I got home I didn't feel well. My mother felt my forehead and noticed that I had a fever. She said, "I'd better coin you to get rid of the bad pressure so you can go to school tomorrow."

Coining is a Cambodian tradition we use to help us feel better when we are sick. A coin is dipped in oil and then its edge is rubbed against the sick person's chest, back, and neck. Coining hurts. This time it hurt so much that my mother had to put her leg on my back so I would stay still. In the end, I felt better inside, but outside I hurt because of the red lines that appeared from the coining.

The next day in class when I went up to ask my teacher about my workbook, she noticed the red marks on my neck and asked me what happened. I tried to explain to her with body language because I couldn't speak well yet. She called someone to take me to the nurse to be examined. The nurse had never seen anything like this before. The principal and the nurse showed me all kinds of objects they thought my parents used to punish me. They thought I was the victim of child abuse. I tried to show them what happened by taking a coin and rubbing it against my arm. They still didn't understand because each red mark was the size of a ruler in width and the marks were deep red like bruises.

values—People's ideas about the worth of certain qualities, such as honesty, hard work, education, respect

get rid of—To make something go away

child abuse—Mistreatment of a child either by beating or by neglect

bruises—Discolored sore places on the skin

The school didn't have an Asian translator. I had never been in a situation like this, and I was afraid of what the people at school would do to me. But they let me call home and I told my parents what happened. Since my parents couldn't speak English, the school called a church agency, which found a Mandarin translator for us.

The translator and my dad went to the school. The people at the school office had angry faces. All my dad could do was explain in detail that coining is a part of our tradition and that we were newcomers. The principal was going to report it to the police, but when he finally understood better what had happened, he dropped the case. He advised my parents not to do coining again. He said that next time I was sick I should stay home and go to a doctor for medicine.

Comprehension

A. *Tell whether these sentences are true or false.*

    1. Wendy's mother wanted Wendy to stay home when she was sick.

    2. Coining is a form of gambling.

    3. Coining hurts.

    4. Coining leaves red marks and bruises on the body.

    5. The school nurse was familiar with coining.

    6. The principal and nurse thought Wendy was a victim of child abuse.

    7. Wendy's father and a translator explained coining to the principal.

    8. The principal told the parents not to do coining again.

B. *Answer these questions.*

    1. Why did Wendy's mother use coining?

    2. Why did Wendy's mom put her leg on Wendy's back?

    3. How is coining done?

    4. Why did the principal want to call the police?

    5. If Wendy ever gets sick again, what does the principal want her to do?

C. *Give your opinion.*

1. Why didn't Wendy know whether to stay home or go to school when she was sick?

2. Why did Wendy's mother use coining instead of taking her to a doctor?

3. Why would Wendy agree to the coining even though she knew it hurt and caused red marks?

4. Did the teacher handle this situation in the best way? What else could she have done?

5. Do you think Wendy's family should give up coining just because the principal told them to? Why or why not?

CULTURE CAPSULE

For certain illnesses like colds and flus, Americans often try home remedies, that is, methods of getting better that do not involve a doctor or medicines. For example, a person might stay in bed, have lots of soup and other liquids, use hot steam to make the air moist, and take lots of vitamin C. Americans also buy over-the-counter medicines like aspirin and cough syrup. Over-the-counter medicines are medicines that do not require a prescription or signed order from a doctor.

For most illnesses, though, Americans go to doctors, who examine them and often write out prescriptions. Home remedies are less common in the United States than in many other parts of the world.

remedies—Treatments or medicines that heal or cure

moist—Slightly wet or damp

Cultural Exchange

A. *Fill in the chart below and then share your answers with your classmates. Look at the following problems. For each problem, write down what you would do in your country and what people do in the United States. You may need to interview some Americans to find out what they do.*

What Do People Do for . . .	Your Country	United States
Fever?		
Cough?		
Diarrhea?		
Rash?		
Back pain?		
Toothache?		
Bleeding?		
A broken bone?		
Burns?		
Childbirth?		
A screaming infant?		

B. *Discuss these questions with your classmates.*

1. In your culture do you have something similar to coining? If so, what do you call it? Describe how it is done.

2. In your country can children go to school if they have a fever, cough, or rash?

3. In your culture are there plants or foods you use to help you get well or keep you from getting sick? Describe.

4. Do you or others in your culture wear anything (around necks, wrists, or waists) to keep from getting sick? Describe.

5. In your culture do people ever pray, chant, or perform rituals when someone is sick? Describe.

6. Do American doctors interact with patients the same way as doctors interact with patients in your country? Explain.

7. Has anything surprised you about the way Americans treat sickness?

Expansion

To increase your vocabulary about medical specialists, solve this crossword puzzle with words from the list below.

cardiologist   ophthalmologist   radiologist

dentist   orthopedist   surgeon

dermatologist   pediatrician   urologist

neurologist   psychiatrist   obstetrician

Across

2 If your baby is sick
7 If you break your arm
9 If you have to have your appendix removed
10 If you have a heart attack
11 If you have a rash
12 If you're going to have a baby

Down

1 If you are having trouble seeing
3 If you need X-rays
4 If you have headaches
5 If you have a toothache
6 If you have trouble urinating
8 If you have emotional problems

 *Role Play*

Work in groups of three. Choose one of the following situations and role-play it for your classmates. Before you role-play, write the conversation.

Situation 1: Role-play "Coining" on pages 16 and 17. Begin your role play when the principal sees Wendy's red marks and bruises.

Use these questions to help you write the conversation:

☐ Is Wendy angry with the principal for misunderstanding or is she embarrassed? Does she want to protect her parents?

☐ Does the principal believe that coining caused the bruises? Does he still suspect the parents?

☐ Is the father confused or angry or embarrassed? Does he feel guilty even though he wasn't trying to harm his daughter?

Student A=Wendy
Student B=the principal
Student C=Wendy's father

After you role-play, discuss these questions with your classmates:

☐ How did Wendy feel about the principal?

☐ How did the principal feel about the father before and after his explanation of coining?

☐ How did the father feel about the school interfering with home health treatments for his child?

Situation 2: A mother and father are at the doctor's office with their seriously ill baby. The doctor says that the baby must have surgery and that the surgery is risky. The parents want to take their baby to a healing shrine where, according to what they have read, the water has miraculously healed thousands of children. The doctor insists that if the surgery is not done immediately, the baby could die. What happens?

shrine—An altar or chapel or special holy place

Continued on the following page

Use these questions to help you write the conversation:

☐ How does the mother feel about the possibility of losing her child either by delaying surgery or by risky surgery?

☐ Is the father angry with the doctor? Does he feel guilty about the risks of delaying surgery?

☐ Does he feel conflict about the healing water because he does not personally know anyone who has been helped?

☐ Does the doctor treat the parents as though they were ignorant? Is he sympathetic? Is he angry?

> Student A=the mother
> Student B=the father
> Student C=the doctor

After you role-play, discuss these questions with your classmates:

☐ Did the doctor try to make the parents feel guilty? Was he sympathetic or cold?

☐ Did the two parents have the same views or was there some disagreement between them?

☐ Were they firm enough in their beliefs about the healing shrine to convince the doctor? Or did they seem uncertain and confused?

☐ What do you think about the way the story ended?

surgery—Medical operation

☐ Do you think that belief in a healing method helps to make it work?

Follow-Up

A. Give a brief oral or written report. Choose number 1 or 2.

1. Tell about a time when you first tried a different healing method and were surprised by the results.

2. Tell about a time when you disagreed with a doctor or other kind of healer.

If you choose number 1, consider including some of the following details:

What was your physical problem? How did this problem come about? When did this happen? Where were you living at the time?

What was the old method you used? What was the new method? Who introduced this new idea to you?

What did you expect to happen? What happened? Why were you surprised?

Did you or would you ever try the method again? Why or why not?

If you choose number 2, consider including some of the following details:

What was your physical problem? How did this problem come about?

When did this happen? Where were you living at the time?

What did the doctor or healer want you to do?

Why did you disagree with this? Were you right to disagree? Why?

What was the response of the doctor or healer? Would you go back to them again? Why or why not? What did you learn from this?

B. *Pick a partner for library research. Then choose and research one of the following topics. Each is a healing method that most doctors* do not *use. Prepare a report for the rest of the class.*

acupuncture	homeopathy
biofeedback	hypnosis
chiropractic	massage
faith healing	midwifery

In your report consider including some of the following details:

What kinds of problems is this method used for? How does it work?

Do many people accept this method? Is there any criticism of it?

Who developed this method?

Do you have anything similar in your culture?

Would you ever consider using this method?

U N I T 4

Food Taboos

? Do you know...

1. Are there any foods Americans do not eat?

2. Has anyone ever refused to eat food you offered them?

Hamburgers

Read the story.

I am Rafael, a second-generation American of Hispanic descent. I was born in Los Angeles and have lived there for eighteen years. My neighborhood is largely Hispanic. Being raised in a community that has one main ethnic group is both good and bad. It is good because I appreciate my culture. It is bad because I am ignorant of other cultures that inhabit the earth. So, not surprisingly, there was an incident when I experienced culture shock. It happened just recently in the home of Gopal, a friend from India.

One rainy day Gopal, who I have known for five months, invited me to his home. On my way there I stopped and bought hamburgers for him and me. However, I did not tell him about the hamburgers.

Gopal's family was eating in the dining room. Gopal and I were in the living room. I asked him, "Do you mind if I eat some food I bought for us?"

"Go right ahead," he answered. "Here, let's go into the dining room. I'll set a place for you at the table."

I seated myself at the table. Slowly I placed the bag on the table and extracted one hamburger for myself and handed the other one to Gopal. As I sank my teeth into the hamburger, his family abruptly stopped eating their meal and began to stare at me. I asked, "Enjoying your meal?"

Not one person answered me. Their stares and the silence that accompanied the stares sent chills through my body. I was confused.

Finally, after about two minutes, Gopal's mother spoke. She said, "You do not know very much about India and our culture. Did you know that in India the cow is considered sacred? It is sacred because the Hindu religion made it holy. We don't and can't eat beef."

She and the family understood that I did not know about Hinduism. I listened and learned more about India. My interest was undivided and her information was rewarding. As a result of this incident I now think before buying beef products. I keep in mind that other

descent—Family origin

ethnic—Cultural, religious, national, or racial group

chills—Unpleasant coldness

sacred—Associated with or dedicated to God or a god

cultures have beliefs that we don't have. I do not think the family, especially Gopal, was affected by the incident. No one was angry at me. It is ironic that Gopal is presently working at Tommy's Burgers.

ironic—unexpected or opposite to what is expected

Comprehension

A. *Tell whether these sentences are true or false.*

1. Rafael was born in Mexico.

2. Gopal was born in India.

3. Rafael and Gopal had been friends since elementary school.

4. Rafael brought hamburgers for himself and Gopal.

5. Gopal's family was offended because of the way Rafael chewed his hamburger.

6. Gopal's mother yelled at Rafael.

7. Rafael was not interested in what Gopal's mother told him.

B. *Answer these questions.*

1. What does Rafael consider bad about living in a community composed of mainly one ethnic group?

2. Why was Gopal's family offended by the hamburgers?

3. How did they react?

4. Why don't Hindus eat beef?

5. How did Rafael accept this information?

6. What kind of job does Gopal now have?

C. *Give your opinion.*

1. How would you describe Rafael's personality and character?

2. Do you think Gopal's mother handled the situation well? Why or why not?

3. Do you think Rafael handled the situation well? Why or why not?

4. What do you think Rafael gained from this experience?

5. If it is taboo for Hindus to eat beef, how do you explain Gopal working at Tommy's Burgers?

CULTURE CAPSULE

From our parents and our culture we learn what is considered good to eat and what is considered bad, what is permitted and what is forbidden. In the United States, no one eats dogs and most people will not eat horse meat. Some foods, although not taboo, are not common either. So some Americans will not eat snails or raw fish, for example.

Certain religious groups have taboos—pork for Jews and Moslems, beef for Hindus. Even individuals may decide not to eat certain foods. People who object to animals being killed may be vegetarians and refuse to eat meat.

forbidden—Not allowed by custom or law

taboo—Something that is forbidden

Cultural Exchange

A. Fill in the chart below and then share your answers with your classmates.

What Are Some Foods That Are . . .	Your Country	United States
Taboo foods?		
Not taboo but not often eaten?		
Favorite main dishes?		
Favorite desserts?		
Favorite snacks?		
Favorite breakfast foods?		
Favorite holiday foods?		

B. *Discuss these questions with your classmates.*

1. What food(s) would you never eat because of religious or family beliefs?

2. When you were a child what food did you refuse to eat that you now like?

3. What new food have you most recently learned to eat?

4. What is your favorite food from your own culture?

5. What is your favorite American food?

6. What American food don't you like?

Expansion

Make a survey of foods that people do not like to eat. Talk to five people outside the classroom. Ask them questions about each of the foods below.

1. Have you ever eaten . . . ?

2. If so, did you like it/them? *or* If not, would you be willing to eat it/them?

   There are four different ways to answer the questions:

   a. Yes, I like to eat it/them.

   b. Yes, but I didn't like it/them.

   c. No, but I'd be willing to eat it/them.

   d. No, and I wouldn't be willing to eat it/them.

   Foods

dog meat	pizza	oysters
horse meat	sheep's eye	beef
snails	raw tomato	brains
raw fish	frog's legs	ants
alligator	bear's paw	beef tongue
hot dogs	calf's liver	snake
milk	animal intestine	pork

3. After you finish your survey, compare your answers with your classmates' answers. Are their answers similar or very different?

Role Play

Work in pairs. Choose one of the following situations and role-play it for your classmates. Before you role-play, write the conversation.

Situation 1: Role-play "Hamburgers" on pages 25 and 26. Begin your role play when Rafael begins to eat his hamburger.

Use these questions to help you write the conversation:

☐ Does Rafael feel surprised or embarrassed when Gopal's family stares at him? Is he apologetic when he learns that he has offended them? Does he feel guilty?

☐ Is Gopal's mother patient with Rafael or is she annoyed?

Student A=Rafael
Student B=Gopal's mother

After you role-play, discuss these questions with your classmates:

☐ Was the mother sensitive to Rafael's ignorance of their customs? Did she feel she had educated him or embarrassed him?

☐ How did Rafael feel after the mother's explanation? Will he be reluctant to visit Gopal's home again?

Situation 2: You are a dinner guest at a friend's home. Your host offers you some food that looks unfamiliar. You accept the food and eat it. Afterwards you ask what the food was and find out it is a food that is taboo for your religion or culture. What happens next?

Use these questions to help you write the conversation:

☐ How does the guest feel upon learning that he or she has eaten a taboo food?

☐ Does the host apologize? Does the host understand the guest's situation? Does the host try to make the guest feel less guilty about breaking the taboo?

☐ Does the guest stay at the friend's house or go home?

Continued on the following page

Student A=the guest

Student B=the host

After you role-play, discuss these questions with your classmates:

☐ How did the guest and the host each react at the dinner?

☐ How did the guest feel the next day?

☐ How did the host feel the next day?

☐ Will the friendship be affected by this incident?

Follow-Up

A. *Give a brief oral or written report. Choose number 1 or 2.*

1. Tell about a time when you were introduced to the most unusual food you ever ate.

2. Tell about a time when you introduced or tried to introduce someone to a food that person had never eaten.

When you describe the event, consider including some of the following details:

How long ago did this happen? How old were you?

Where were you living at the time?

Describe the occasion (a meal at home? a meal in a restaurant? a simple meal? a family banquet?)

Describe the food. How was it prepared?

What did the food look like? How did it taste?

If you choose number 1, also consider including some of the following details:

Did someone have to convince you to eat the food? Did you enjoy it or not?

Have you ever eaten it again? Would you ever eat it again? If not, why not?

If you choose number 2, also consider including some of the following details:

Why hadn't the other person ever eaten this food?

Did the other person try the food? If so, did he or she enjoy it?

If the other person would not eat the food, how did you feel about that?

Did this experience affect your relationship with the other person in any way? If so, how?

B. *Create a one-page advertisement for your favorite food. Use colorful words to describe how it tastes, looks, and makes you feel when you eat it. You can also include a drawing to show how good it looks.*

Pin or tape your advertisement to the wall with your classmates' advertisements. How many of you chose the same foods?

U N I T 5

Eating Out

? Do you know...

1. In the United States which foods can be eaten without using any utensils?

2. Have you ever been confused about which utensil to use or how to use it?

Eating the Western Way

Read the story.

I was born in Vietnam and since both of my parents are Chinese, most of the things I do are based on Chinese customs. However, I have lived in the United States for a long time so I have also picked up many American ways, but I still use my Chinese name, Yen.

The one thing I find very difficult to get used to is the eating utensils. In many American restaurants there are two forks, two spoons, and two knives. I get really confused trying to find out which utensil I should use for which kind of food. And not long ago, I didn't know how to use a knife and fork at all.

In my culture the two items we use for eating are a pair of chopsticks and a soup spoon. Chopsticks are long skinny sticks made out of wood called bamboo. We use them to pick up our food. The soup spoon is oval in shape and is usually made out of porcelain. We use it to sip our soup or to scoop our food.

Two years ago, my boyfriend invited me to the Christmas party given by his company. He told me that it was going to be a dinner party at the Sheraton Hotel and that I should dress formally. The week before the party, I went shopping for a pretty dress to wear. I had a hard time because I didn't really know how Americans would dress for this occasion. Well, luckily for me, a salesgirl gave me her opinion and I found just the right dress. Then came the day of the party. Knowing I was properly dressed, I felt very comfortable. My boyfriend introduced me to his co-workers, and we were seated at a table with four other American couples. Then I looked down at my knife and fork, and my heart sank. I had wanted to ask my boyfriend how to use the utensils for what I called "Eating the Western Way." But I had been so worried about what to wear that I had forgotten. Now, seated at the table with the other couples, I would have to

utensils—Objects that are used to cut and eat food

porcelain—A thin, shiny material of very fine quality that is produced by baking a clay mixture

figure out the utensils for myself. Everything went fine until the lady who was sitting next to me noticed that I kept watching what everyone was doing and switching my fork and knife from one hand to another. She started to laugh and said, "Oh dear, don't be so nervous. Let me show you how to use your knife."

At this point my face was red and I didn't know what to say. Usually Chinese people aren't allowed to have a knife on the table. I was still a little scared to hold the knife and now I was also nervous and embarrassed about the whole situation. I ended up letting my boyfriend cut the steak for me. As for the lady who was sitting next to me, I was too embarrassed to look at her or thank her for offering to help.

Since then, my boyfriend has taken me to many American restaurants. Not only have I gotten used to eating the food, but he has taught me how to eat the Western way. Now I have no problem handling my knife and fork, but it makes me smile sometimes when I think of how embarrassing it once was.

Comprehension

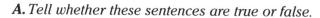

A. *Tell whether these sentences are true or false.*

1. Yen has had trouble getting used to American utensils.

2. In Yen's culture two kinds of utensils are used for eating.

3. Yen had no trouble shopping for a formal dress.

4. The salesgirl was rude to Yen.

5. The lady next to Yen at the dinner tried to help her.

6. Yen let the lady help her.

7. Yen's boyfriend cut her steak.

8. Now Yen has no problem handling her knife and fork.

B. *Answer these questions.*

1. What does Yen find confusing about the utensils in American restaurants?

2. What utensils are used in Yen's culture?

3. Where was the dinner party held?

4. How did Yen feel about the dress she wore?

5. What is "Eating the Western Way"?

6. How did Yen learn to become good at eating the Western way?

C. *Give your opinion.*

1. When the lady at the table laughed at Yen do you think she was making fun of her?

2. How do you think the lady felt when Yen did not thank her for her offer of help?

3. Do you think it was kind of the lady to help or do you think she was interfering?

4. Do you think Yen's boyfriend was right to cut her steak for her? Why or why not?

5. If you were in Yen's place, what would you have done that night?

CULTURE CAPSULE

In American homes table settings usually just include a fork, a knife, and a small spoon (teaspoon). In some restaurants, though, there may be two of each kind of utensil—one large and one small. There is a small spoon for stirring coffee or tea and a larger spoon for soup. The large fork and knife are for the main course. The small fork is for salad or dessert, while the small knife is for buttering bread. For some foods there are special utensils—for example, a very small fork for shellfish and a spoon with a sharp edge for grapefruit.

Usually, it is the more elegant restaurants that use a lot of utensils. Many restaurants have only the basic knife, fork, and spoon, and at places that sell pizza people usually do not use any utensils at all.

Cultural Exchange

A. *Fill in the chart below and then share your answers with your classmates.*

In a Restaurant . . .	Your Country	United States
What foods can be eaten with fingers?		
How do people get the food server's attention?		
How do people express appreciation for the meal? (sounds? words?)		
What words do people say to make a toast?		
Do people leave the food server a tip?		
Do people ever split the check?		

make a toast—To drink and wish out loud for success and happiness

tip—Money left for food servers by satisfied customers—usually 15–20% of the check

split the check—To divide the bill equally among the people eating, or each person pays his or her own share

B. *Discuss these questions with your classmates.*

1. What does a typical table setting look like in your culture? On a piece of paper, draw plates, bowls, drinking glasses or cups, and utensils in their usual positions. Explain the table setting to your classmates.

2. In your culture where do you sit when you eat? (on the floor? on pillows? on chairs?)

3. In your culture are there foods you are allowed to eat while standing or walking? What foods are they? In the United States what foods would you eat while standing or walking?

4. In your culture are children taken out to eat with adults? If so, how are the children expected to behave? What have you observed about children eating out in the United States? Do parents often seem to take children out to eat? How do the children behave?

5. In your country did you eat out? If so, in what kinds of places did you eat out? Do you eat out in the United States? Where?

Expansion

Draw a line from the food in the left-hand column to the appropriate description in the right-hand column.

Brownie	Ground beef with chili sauce poured over a roll
Caesar salad	Bread dipped in egg batter and then fried
Club sandwich	A large cut of beef cooked for a long time with vegetables in a liquid
Fish sticks	Lettuce with anchovies, with a dressing of lemon juice, seasonings, olive oil, and raw egg, and with bread croutons and Parmesan cheese on top
French toast	Fish filets cut in finger shapes, breaded, and fried
Hot dog	A rich chocolate cake square, often with nuts inside
Pancakes	Meat sausage in a bun, often eaten with mustard and relish
Sloppy joe	Cold meats and cheese, often with lettuce, tomatoes, peppers, and seasonings, served on a long roll
Submarine (Hero) sandwich	A three-layered toasted sandwich, often filled with chicken or turkey, lettuce, tomatoes, and bacon
Waldorf salad	Flat fried cakes, often eaten with syrup
Pot roast	Cut-up apples, celery, and nuts mixed in a mayonnaise dressing

Role Play

Work in groups of three. Choose one of the following situations and role-play it for your classmates. Before you role-play, write the conversation.

Situation 1: Role-play "Eating the Western Way" on pages 33 and 34. Begin your role play when Yen is having difficulties and the lady sitting next to her offers to help.

Continued on the following page

Use these questions to help you write the conversation:

☐ Is Yen embarrassed by the lady's offer to cut her meat or is she grateful that someone recognized her problem? Is she embarrassed or relieved when her boyfriend cuts the meat?

☐ Is the boyfriend grateful to the lady for her offer or is he resentful? What makes him cut Yen's meat?

☐ Is the lady angry or disappointed when Yen does not look at her and will not let her help? Or does she understand how Yen feels?

☐ Do Yen and/or her boyfriend finally talk to the lady?

> Student A=Yen
> Student B=Yen's boyfriend
> Student C=the lady sitting next to Yen

After you role-play, discuss these questions with your classmates:

☐ How did Yen feel when her boyfriend cut her meat?

☐ How did the lady feel about Yen?

☐ How did the boyfriend feel about Yen? Did he feel sorry for her? Was he embarrassed or angry?

> **Situation 2:** An Arabic friend invites an American to a dinner his father is giving in an Arabic restaurant. The American friend is shocked to discover he must eat with his fingers. He has never done this before. He asks his friend if he might ask for a fork and knife. The friend says that although the restaurant has forks and knives, this would offend his father. Write the ending to the story.

Use these questions to help you write the conversation:

☐ Is the father angry with his son for inviting an outsider or is he pleased?

☐ If the guest refuses to eat with his fingers, is the father angry? If the guest follows the Arabic custom, is the father pleased?

☐ If the American rejects the Arabic custom, how does the friend react? If the American follows the custom, how does the friend react?

☐ If the guest agrees to use his fingers is he embarrassed or does he find out he likes using his fingers? Is he angry that he was not told about this custom ahead of time?

Student A=the Arabic friend

Student B=the American friend

Student C=the father

After you role-play, discuss these questions with your classmates:

☐ How did the two friends feel about each other by the end of the evening? How might this experience affect the friendship?

☐ How did the father feel regarding his son's choice of a friend?

☐ How did the Arabic boy feel about his father? Was he proud or was he resentful that his father would want his friend to follow the Arabic custom?

☐ Did the American seem open to learning new customs? Why or why not?

Follow-Up

A. *Give a brief oral or written report. Choose number 1 or 2.*

1. Tell about a time when you were eating in a restaurant and something was wrong with the food and you did something about it.

2. Tell about a time in a restaurant when you found something wrong with the check and you did something about it.

When you describe the event, consider including some of the following details:

When did this happen?

Where were you living at the time?

What was the restaurant called?

What was wrong with the food or the check?

What did you do about it?

What did the restaurant do about it?

Were you satisfied with the results?

Have you ever returned to that restaurant?

B. *Ordering at the restaurant: Collect some menus from local restaurants. Work in groups of three to five. One person is the food server who takes the order and makes* *out the check. The rest of the group are the customers who order the food, check the bill, and figure out the 15 percent tip. You can ask for individual checks or you may want to practice "splitting the check." Here are typical food-server questions and responses:*

"Are you ready to order?"

"What would you like this evening?"

"Hi. My name is _____. May I bring you something to drink before you order?"

"Will there be anything else?"

"Thank you and come again."

Here are typical questions and responses from customers:

"What's today's special?"

"Is there anything you would recommend?"

"We're ready to order now."

"May we have our check?"

special—In a restaurant, food not regularly offered or food that has a lower price than usual

UNIT 6

Guests and Hosts

? Do you know…

1. What do you usually bring to someone's home if you are invited for dinner?

2. What is a potluck meal?

Potluck

Read the story.

My name is Tai and I was born in the southern part of China. After receiving a B.A. degree, I taught English in Beijing and later became an interpreter. Now I am in the United States to get a degree in marketing.

When I first came to this country, everything seemed strange and different. For example, people often said hello to each other even if they were strangers. In China, only friends say hello when they meet. But, of all the cultural differences, one in particular came as a surprise to me. An American friend invited me to a dinner party at her home. A day before the party, I happened to talk to a Chinese friend. He asked me what food I was bringing to the party. I had no idea what he was talking about. In China, the hosts prepare all the food and drinks—the only thing that the guests bring is their mouths to eat with. My friend explained to me that the dinner party was a potluck. He said that at a potluck dinner party each guest brings food and everybody shares the food. It was lucky that I talked to this friend before the dinner. I had just planned to bring a bottle of liquor, and I would have felt embarrassed. Instead, I made some typical Chinese food for the potluck, and everyone there really liked it.

As I've learned, many dinners in the United States aren't potlucks. They are more like our Chinese dinners. Guests may bring a bottle of wine or a small gift, but the hosts provide the meal. However, I've also come to like the custom of potlucks. Since everyone helps out, potlucks make it easy to have dinner with friends more often. This is especially useful since so many women today work and have less time to cook large meals. By now I've explained this custom to many Chinese friends here. And when I'm invited to a potluck, I always do my best to bring some typical Chinese food.

potluck—A type of meal to which each guest brings food to share

B.A. degree—Bachelor of Arts certificate, usually received after completing four years of college courses

interpreter—A person who puts the words of one language into the words of another language, usually by talking

marketing—How goods are advertised and sold

UNIT 6 *Guests and Hosts*

Comprehension

A. *Tell whether these sentences are true or false.*

1. In China, only friends say hello to each other when they meet.

2. Tai was planning to give a dinner party.

3. He did not know what *potluck* meant.

4. *Potluck* is the name of a delicious Chinese food.

5. In China, hosts provide all the food and drink.

6. In the United States, hosts often provide all the food and drink.

7. Tai does not like potlucks.

8. Americans do not like potluck dinner parties because they are too much work.

B. *Answer these questions.*

1. What does *potluck* mean?

2. Who explained potluck to Tai?

3. Originally, what did Tai plan to bring to the party?

4. What is the Chinese custom for dinner parties?

5. What kind of food does Tai like to bring to potlucks?

6. Who has Tai explained the potluck custom to?

C. *Give your opinion.*

1. Tai says that for him potlucks were one of the most surprising American customs. Do you find the custom of potluck surprising? What American customs have surprised you the most?

2. Tai says he would have been very embarrassed if he had gone to the potluck without food. Do you agree that this would have been embarrassing? Explain your answer.

3. Have you ever been to a potluck? Which do you prefer—potlucks or regular dinner parties where the hosts do all the work?

4. How do you think Tai's Chinese friends react when he explains potluck to them? Why do you think so?

5. Do you think Tai has a positive or negative attitude about living in a new culture? Explain.

CULTURE CAPSULE

Although friends and neighbors sometimes "drop in," usually Americans do not visit one another without an invitation. If you are invited to someone's home for dinner, the invitation might be only for you and your spouse. Do not bring your children or parents unless they were invited or you have asked the host. Do not arrive earlier than the time mentioned and try not to be too late.

You might ask your hosts if you can bring something. If they say no, then you can still bring a small gift—for example, flowers, a box of candy, or a bottle of wine. If you are invited to a potluck, of course, you are expected to bring some food.

spouse—A person's husband or wife

Cultural Exchange

A. Fill in the chart below and then share your answers with your classmates.

If People Are Invited to Dinner . . .	Your Country	United States
Who do they usually bring?		
When do they arrive? (at the time the host mentioned? 30 minutes late? early? other?)		
What do they bring the host?		
When do they start eating? (as soon as they get there? a short time later?)		
What do they do if the the food is delicious? (say something? to whom?)		
If they are hungry and the host offers more food, do they first say yes or do they first say no?		
What is one thing people should never do at the table?		
When do people leave? (right after eating? about an hour after eating? other?)		
What do people say when leaving?		

B. *Discuss these questions with your classmates.*

1. In your culture do guests offer to help serve the food or clear the table?

2. In your culture what are some favorite topics of conversation at dinner parties? After dinner, do the women and men tend to break up into separate groups?

3. In your culture who usually cooks the food for a dinner party?

4. In your culture is alcohol served at dinner parties? If so, what kind? If not, what do people drink with the meal?

5. Would you say that dinner parties in the United States are basically similar to dinner parties in your country or quite different? What are the biggest differences?

Expansion

Draw a line from the word or words in the left-hand column to the appropriate definition in the right-hand column.

Barbecue	Small amounts of food that generally accompany drinks before dinner; for example, tiny sandwiches, chips, and dips
Black tie event	Drinking in honor of the host or a guest; glasses are raised as words of praise are said
Brunch	Generally held outdoors, in a backyard or in a park; food is cooked over hot coals
Grace	A party to which men and women must wear formal clothes; for example, a man would wear a dinner jacket and tie or a tuxedo
Hors d'oeuvres (appetizers)	Each guest brings some food to the meal
BYOB	You must let the host know whether or not you plan to attend
Potluck	You only have to let your host know if you are not coming to the party
Regrets Only	Bring you own bottle of wine or something to drink
RSVP	A combination meal of breakfast and lunch usually served between 11:00 a.m. and 1:00 p.m.
Toasts	A short prayer spoken aloud or silently just before food is eaten

Role Play

Work in pairs. Choose one of the following situations and role-play it for your classmates. Before you role-play, write the conversation.

Situation 1: A dinner guest arrives late at his friend's home and has brought his two children and his wife's parents. The host tries to welcome them but he is upset by the lateness and by the extra guests, and he knows that his wife is also very annoyed. The guest notices that the table is set for only four people, and he is also aware that his friend is acting strangely.

Use these questions to help you write the conversation:

☐ Will the guest ask his friend what is wrong? If his friend tells him, what will he do or say? Will he tell the host that customs are different in his country? Will he be casual about it or apologetic?

☐ Will the host tell his friend what he has done wrong? Will he ignore it and just set some extra places at the table? Will he be friendly to the friend's parents and children?

Student A=the guest
Student B=the host

After you role-play, discuss these questions with your classmates:

☐ What were the host's and guest's first reactions to the situation? What did they do? Do you think they should have done anything differently?

☐ At the end of the role play, how do the host and guest each feel?

Situation 2: Two friends bump into each other at the supermarket. One is an American, the other is from another country. The American asks the friend over for dinner that night. The friend is hesitant at first but finally accepts and asks for the address and time.

Use these questions to help you write the conversation:

☐ Is the friend hesistant because he or she is worried about food or other customs? Or is there some other reason for the hesitation? Is this the first time the person has been invited to an American home?

☐ Does the American understand the friend's hesitation? How does the American convince the friend to come over?

> Student A=the American friend
> Student B=the friend from another country

After you role-play, discuss these questions with your classmates:

☐ Why was the non-American friend at first reluctant to accept the invitation? How did the American persuade the other person to accept the invitation?

☐ Once the invitation was accepted, how do you think the two friends felt?

☐ How did you feel the first time you invited someone from another culture to visit your home?

☐ How did you feel the first time you were invited to the home of someone from another culture?

Follow-Up

A. *Give a brief oral or written report. Choose number 1 or 2.*

1. Tell about a time when you hosted a meal and one of your guests did something surprising.

2. Tell about a time when you were a guest at a party and either you or one of the other guests did something that was embarrassing.

In your report, consider including some of the following details:
When did this happen?
Where were you living at the time?
What was your role? (guest or host)
What was the occasion?
What went wrong?
How did you react?
How did others react?
Did anyone learn anything from this experience? Explain.

B. *Write a thank-you note to someone who invited you to a dinner party. It was an elegant dinner party, and you really enjoyed it because your host paid special attention to you and made you feel welcome.*

UNIT 7
Confusing Phrases

Do you know...

1. What does it mean when someone is "pulling your leg" or when someone asks you to "shake a leg" or tells you to "break a leg"?

2. What other American phrases have confused you?

Quit Pulling My Leg

Read the story.

My name is Lorenzo and I was born in Mexico City, but I've been living here in the United States for five years. While in the tenth grade I had an incident with my ESL teacher, Mrs. Del Signore.

It all began one night when I stayed up until midnight doing homework for the next day. When I finished, I put the homework paper on the dinner table and went to sleep. The next morning I woke up late and was in such a hurry to get to school on time that I forgot to take my homework.

In my ESL class, Mrs. Del Signore said, "Pass your homework to the front of your row." Today, like every day, she used the homework to take attendance. So, after a few minutes, she asked, "Lorenzo Gonzales is not here?" I answered, "I'm here."

She turned and looked at me and called me to her desk to ask me about the homework. When I explained what had happened, she answered, "Quit pulling my leg. I want the truth."

I felt my face turning red. What she said didn't make any sense. I wasn't close enough to pull her leg. Besides, she was sitting at her desk, and it would have been practically impossible to pull her leg from under the desk. The whole class looked at her because they did not understand her either. I'm sure I had a perplexed look on my face. When Mrs. Del Signore noticed it, she immediately realized the reason and apologized to me and the rest of the class. She explained what she meant by "pulling my leg." She had thought I was kidding her about the homework, that I was just making up a story.

The next day she discussed idioms. We were eager to learn them, since we could clearly see they would come in handy sooner or later. As a result of this experience, to this day whenever I hear an idiom I do not understand, I simply go to my old high school and ask my friend Mrs. Del Signore.

perplexed—Confused

kidding—Teasing or deceiving in a playful way

come in handy—To be useful or convenient

Comprehension

A. *Tell whether these sentences are true or false.*

1. Lorenzo forgot to do his ESL homework.

2. Lorenzo overslept the next morning.

3. Mrs. Del Signore uses the homework to take attendance.

4. Lorenzo could not really pull Mrs. Del Signore's leg, because she was sitting at her desk.

5. Lorenzo was the only student who did not understand what his teacher meant.

6. "Pulling a leg" is an idiom that means to arrive late.

7. Lorenzo likes Mrs. Del Signore.

B. *Answer these questions.*

1. Why did Lorenzo forget his homework?

2. What was Lorenzo's reaction when his teacher said, "Quit pulling my leg"?

3. What does "Quit pulling my leg" mean?

4. What did Mrs. Del Signore do to help her students?

5. What does Lorenzo do now when he does not understand an idiom?

C. *Give your opinion.*

1. Do you think Lorenzo is a good student? Why?

2. Do you think Mrs. Del Signore is a good teacher? Why?

3. What do you think Mrs. Del Signore learned from this experience?

4. Suppose your teacher used an idiom you did not understand. What would you do? What would you do if a friend used an idiom you did not understand?

CULTURE CAPSULE

There are many idioms about legs in American English. "Pulling someone's leg" means not telling that person the truth. To "shake a leg" means to hurry, and if someone tells you to "break a leg," it means he or she is wishing you good luck.

Other parts of the body are also frequently used in idioms. "Don't lose your head" means to stay calm. To have "sticky fingers" means to steal. To "win by a hair" means to barely win, and if someone says "you're wet behind the ears," it means you lack experience.

Cultural Exchange

A. *Here is a list of idioms and their meanings. What do you have in your language that is comparable?*

Idiom	Meaning	Your Language
A long face	To be sad	
Let your hair down	Relax	
Pain in the neck	Someone or something that causes a problem	
Face the music	Confront an issue	
Get off someone's back	Stop bothering a person	
Keep an eye on	Watch	
Heart of gold	To be generous	

B. *Discuss these questions with your classmates.*

1. What American idioms seem especially interesting to you?

2. Which American idioms are difficult for you to understand?

3. Which American idioms do you use?

4. Do you often use idioms from your native language? Which ones?

5. Are there American idioms that correspond to the ones you use in your own language?

Expansion

Choose one of the following idioms or proverbs or think of one of your own. Draw a picture of what the idiom or proverb describes. Then show the drawing to your classmates to determine whether they know which idiom or proverb you have drawn and what it really means.

He's a chip off the old block.

The cold shoulder

It's raining cats and dogs.

Out of the frying pan into the fire

Kill two birds with one stone

Getting ripped off

Don't bite the hand that feeds you.

Hit the nail on the head

Money is burning a hole in your pocket.

He's a wolf in sheep's clothing.

Bury the hatchet

 *Role Play*

Work in pairs. Choose one of the following situations and role-play it for your classmates. Before you role-play, write the conversation.

Situation 1: Role-play "Quit Pulling My Leg" on page 49. Begin your role play when Mrs. Del Signore asks whether Lorenzo is in class. Have her use the idiom, as in the story. See if you can come up with a different ending.

Use these questions to help you write the conversation:

☐ Is Mrs. Del Signore angry with Lorenzo for not having his homework? Is she sympathetic or impatient?

☐ Does Lorenzo feel frightened or guilty when Mrs. Del Signore calls him to her desk? Is he embarrassed about leaving his work at home?

☐ How does Lorenzo feel when Mrs. Del Signore accuses him of pulling her leg? What does he say or do?

Student A=Lorenzo
Student B=Mrs. Del Signore

After you role-play, discuss these questions with your classmates:

☐ Does Mrs. Del Signore seem like a nice teacher? How would you describe Mrs. Del Signore?

☐ Does Lorenzo seem like a hard-working student? How would you describe Lorenzo?

☐ Did Mrs. Del Signore believe Lorenzo in the end? How did they clear up the confusion about the idiom?

Situation 2: The International Students Club is giving a party for its new members. Amy, the president of the club, is upset because people are not talking to one another. She asks her advisor what she should do, and the advisor tells Amy that she needs to go and break the ice. The advisor is surprised when she sees Amy walk to the refreshment table, pick up a knife, and start chipping the ice in the ice bucket. The advisor then realizes that Amy does not know what "break the ice" means. (It means to make people more relaxed and sociable.) Write the ending to this story.

Use these questions to help you write the conversation:

☐ How does Amy feel before the party begins?

☐ How does Amy feel when the guests do not talk to one another?

☐ How does Amy feel about asking her advisor for help?

☐ How will the advisor respond when Amy comes to her for help?

☐ How will she respond when she discovers Amy chipping the ice in the ice bucket? Will she laugh at her? Will she be understanding?

☐ Will the advisor feel apologetic about using the idiom? What does she do about it?

> Student A=Amy
> Student B=the advisor

After you role-play, discuss these questions with your classmates:

☐ How did Amy feel after she discovered the real meaning of "break the ice"?

☐ Was Amy angry with her advisor? Was she embarrassed or did she laugh at her own mistake?

☐ Did the advisor feel guilty about causing Amy this embarrassment?

☐ How did the party guests react to the incident? Did it help to break the ice?

☐ How can the advisor turn this incident into a positive learning experience for the international students?

Follow-Up

A. Give a brief oral or written report. Choose number 1 or 2.

1. Tell about a time when you misunderstood the meaning of words in your own language or another language.

2. Tell about a time when something you said was misunderstood by someone else.

In your report, consider including some of the following details:

When did this happen? How old were you?

Where were you living at the time?

Continued on the following page

Who was the person that was confused?

In what language was the misunderstood phrase? Was it a difference in language?

What was the misunderstood phrase?

What was the real meaning of the words?

What did you or the other person think the words meant?

How did the person who misunderstood react?

What happened as a result of the misunderstanding?

How did the misunderstanding get cleared up?

B. *Work with two other students and make a list of American phrases that have caused you some confusion. Compare your list with those of your classmates.*

U nit 8

Greetings

 ## Do you know...

1. How do friends in the United States greet each other?

2. How do Americans greet one another in business settings?

Hand Kissing

Read the story.

My name is Cristina. I was born in Mexico and came to the United States when I was three months old. Even though we lived in the United States, my parents raised my brother, my sisters, and me just as they had been raised in Mexico—with very strict rules. My parents taught us we should respect grandparents more than anyone in the world because grandparents had lived the longest. They had more knowledge about life, and no matter what they said, even if it didn't make sense, they were right. We were taught that to hug or kiss grandparents was disrespectful and that we should greet them by kissing their hand. When you are young, you think that everyone lives and thinks just like you do. Well, I soon found out this isn't true.

My best friend in third grade was the first close friend I had who was raised in the American way. This friend invited me to her birthday party. I was very excited because I had never been invited to a friend's birthday party before.

The day of the party came, and I was happy but at the same time very nervous. I thought of all the people who would be there. I wanted her family to like me. Slowly, I walked up to the house. Finally, I got to the door and rang the bell. My friend came running out with a big smile, telling me she was happy that I came. She let me in and introduced me to her parents. They smiled and said hello. Then she said, "Come here. I want you to meet my grandpa."

I followed her into the living room where her grandfather was sitting. She introduced us and he reached out his hand. He was going to shake hands, but I thought he was expecting me to kiss his hand, so I did.

I noticed that he looked at me in a strange way, as if he didn't like what I had done. Everyone else in the room looked at me, and my friend started laughing. I was very confused. I didn't know what I had done wrong. I sat down and tried to figure out what

strict—Severe; requiring complete obedience

happened. Just then, a little boy ran to my friend's grandfather and jumped on his lap. The little boy started to hug and kiss the grandfather. When I saw this, I got up and took the little boy by the hand and said, "No." I guess I said it pretty loudly because the room became very silent and all eyes were on me. The next day at school my friend asked me why I acted so strange at her party. She asked me why I kissed her grandfather's hand and why I told the little boy to get away from his grandfather. I explained my customs to her and she explained hers to me. Fortunately, we stayed very good friends.

Comprehension

A. *Tell whether these sentences are true or false.*

1. Cristina had very many American friends.

2. Cristina's parents let their children follow whatever customs they desired.

3. In Cristina's culture grandparents were highly respected because they had lived the longest and knew the most.

4. Cristina loved to hug and kiss her grandparents.

5. At the party the grandfather was surprised when Cristina kissed his hand.

6. The little boy kissed the grandfather's hand too.

7. The party guests were very surprised by Cristina's behavior.

8. Cristina's friend would not have anything to do with her after this incident.

B. *Answer these questions.*

1. Why couldn't Cristina hug or kiss her grandparents?

2. What was the correct form when greeting them?

3. What kind of greeting was her friend's grandfather used to getting from his grandchildren?

4. What kind of greeting did he expect from Cristina?

5. Why did Cristina say "No" to the little boy?

6. Why did the room become silent?

C. Give your opinion.

1. Why do you think Cristina's parents continued to follow their Mexican traditions even though they lived in the United States?

2. Do you think Cristina's parents made a good decision about keeping their Mexican traditions? Why or why not?

3. To help ease the situation, what might the grandfather have said to Cristina after she kissed his hand?

4. What do you think the party guests thought about Cristina?

5. Do you think it was a good idea for Cristina's girlfriend to ask her why she acted so strange at the party? Why or why not?

CULTURE CAPSULE

In the United States the form of greeting depends on how well people know each other and on the situation. When people are first introduced, they usually shake hands. Handshakes are especially common in business or formal situations.

When two women friends meet, they might hug and kiss one another on the cheek. (Although in many cultures, people kiss on both cheeks, Americans usually just kiss on one cheek.) Male friends would not kiss but might embrace for a moment. A male friend and female friend might kiss on the cheek, even though they are not romantically involved. If people know each other but not well, they might just say hello. Friends often do this, too. A stranger might greet an older person with a handshake. A grandchild would probably greet his or her grandparents with hugs and kisses.

embrace—To hold closely and affectionately in one's arms; to hug

romantically involved—In a love relationship; boyfriend and girlfriend

Cultural Exchange

A. *Compare the way you greet people in your own country with the way Americans greet one another. Fill in the chart, for example, with pat on arm, slap on the back, bow, hug, kiss, nod, handshake, and then share your answers with your classmates.*

How Do People Greet . . .	Your Country	United States
Parents?		
Brothers and sisters?		
Grandparents?		
A boss?		
A spouse?		
A sweetheart?		
A friend of the same sex?		
A friend of the opposite sex?		

B. *Discuss these questions with your classmates.*

1. In your culture, how do you greet a stranger?

2. In your culture, what are the rules for handshaking? Must you use a firm grip? Do women shake hands with women? Do women shake hands with men?

3. In your culture, what is the meaning of a smile? Do you smile at strangers? at friends?

4. What do you find difficult to get used to about American greeting customs?

5. Do you prefer the greeting customs in your culture or in American culture? Or do you prefer some from each culture? Explain your answer.

Expansion

With one or two partners, practice some American greetings for the following situations. Then perform the greeting for your classmates. Some examples of words you might use to go along with the greetings are given below. You can also make up your own.

1. Good friends who have not seen each other in a few weeks
2. Co-workers who unexpectedly see each other at the shopping mall
3. An aunt greeting her niece
4. A boss introducing a new employee to other employees

"Hello, how are you?"

"I'm fine, thank you."

"You look wonderful."

"I'm pleased to meet you."

"I've really missed you."

 *Role Play*

Work in pairs. Choose one of the following situations and role-play it for your classmates. Before you role-play, write the conversation.

Situation 1: Role-play "Hand Kissing" on pages 56 and 57. Begin your role play the day after the party, at school, when Cristina's friend asks her about her strange behavior.

Use these questions to help you write the conversation:

☐ What might have happened at the party after Cristina kissed the grandfather's hand and pulled the boy from the grandfather's lap?

☐ Did Cristina stay at the party or did she feel embarrassed and leave early? If she stayed, how did her friend and the other people at the party treat her?

☐ Is Cristina today still confused or angry about the behavior of the grandfather, the boy, the party guests, and her friend?

☐ Is Cristina's friend sorry she invited her? Is she worried about what her family thinks about her choice of friends?

After you role-play, discuss these questions with your classmates:

☐ What attitude does the friend have about Cristina's different customs? What is her attitude toward Cristina now?

☐ Does Cristina feel embarrassed about her behavior? Will she still remain proud of her own customs?

> **Situation 2:** Lan has just arrived from Hong Kong, and it is her first day in an American school. Her new teacher, Mr. Allen, introduces her to the other students, who all say "Hi." In return, Lan bows to Mr. Allen and then to her classmates, but they laugh at her for bowing and she becomes very embarrassed. What happens after that? Write the ending to this story.

Use these questions to help you write the conversation:

☐ Does Mr. Allen first talk to his students or to Lan? What can he say or do to make Lan feel less embarrassed? Does he scold the students or give them an explanation about greeting customs? Is there something else he might do?

☐ Is Lan angry with the students or is she angry with Mr. Allen for letting the students laugh at her? How does this make her feel about her own greeting customs?

> Student A=Lan
> Student B=Mr. Allen

After you role-play, discuss these questions with your classmates:

☐ Was Mr. Allen able to smooth over the situation? Do his students feel apologetic?

☐ How can Mr. Allen prevent this kind of classroom situation from occurring in the future?

☐ What is Lan's attitude toward her classmates?

☐ What is Lan's attitude toward Mr. Allen?

☐ Will Lan want to change her bowing habits? If so, how difficult will this be?

Follow-Up

A. *Give a brief oral or written report. Choose number 1 or 2.*

1. Tell about a time when you were greeted in a very unexpected way or were expected to greet someone in a way that was difficult for you.

2. Tell about a time when you observed a greeting custom that was different.

In your report, consider including some of the following details:

When did it happen?

How old were you?

Where were you living at the time?

What were the cultural backgrounds of the people involved?

What greeting behavior was expected?

Describe the greeting. What was different about it?

How did those individuals involved react to the situation?

B. *Write a letter to a friend from your culture who is planning to visit the United States. Give some good advice about the accepted greeting customs. Are there any greeting customs from your culture that might be misunderstood in the United States? Tell your friend to avoid these greeting customs.*

Forms of Address

? Do you know...

1. What kinds of people would you address by their first name? What kinds of people would you address by a title (Mr., Ms., etc.) and last name?

2. How are teachers addressed in the United States?

What Should I Call You?

Read the story.

My name is Yuan. As a student in Taiwan for the first ten years of my school life, I learned to respect teachers. I was taught that it is not respectful to call teachers by their name, that they should always be addressed by the title "teacher."

Seven years ago, when I moved to the United States, I entered an ESL class in a local high school. The students kept calling the teacher "Miss White." I felt that they were being disrespectful, but because of my problems with English, I couldn't ask them about it.

Time passed. I found that often when I asked questions, Miss White seemed annoyed and said something, but I was not able to understand what she said. I wondered if I had done something that was not respectful or if somehow I hadn't been a good student. Finally, one day when I raised my hand and said, "Excuse me, teacher . . . ," Miss White interrupted me before I could finish my question. With a not-so-happy face, she said, "Teacher is my title at work. Teacher is not my name. My name is Miss White."

Now I was completely confused. Why would she want me to call her by her name? Why would she get so upset when I was trying to be respectful? I wanted to ask her the reason but my English was still not good enough.

I was angry and sad for a few days, until my uncle returned from Taiwan. I asked him, "Why do people get upset simply because I am trying to respect them?" He asked me to tell him the whole story. I told him what happened in school. He told me that what was right back in Taiwan was not necessarily proper here in the United States. He also told me that I should not be sad and that I should try to understand what is done here and avoid making the same mistakes.

disrespectful—Not respectful

proper—Correct, appropriate, acceptable

After the incident, when I'm not sure what to do, I observe other people and do things the way they do. Even though this sometimes makes me feel that I am not being myself, it helps me avoid a lot of cultural difficulties. Of course, now I am also able to ask people questions. As I learn more, life here becomes much more interesting and enjoyable.

Comprehension

A. Tell whether these sentences are true or false.

1. Yuan was confused when the students called the teacher "Miss White."

2. Yuan asked the students why they did this but they would not tell her.

3. In Taiwan the respectful way to address teachers is to call them "teacher."

4. Miss White was annoyed when Yuan called her "teacher."

5. Yuan also felt very annoyed at Miss White.

6. Yuan discussed the misunderstanding with Miss White.

7. Yuan's uncle laughed at Yuan.

8. Yuan does not enjoy American culture anymore.

B. Answer these questions.

1. Why did Yuan think it was disrespectful to call her teacher "Miss White"?

2. Why did Miss White get mad at Yuan?

3. Why didn't Yuan ask her classmates about the problem?

4. What did Yuan's uncle tell her?

5. What does Yuan do now when she is not sure about what to do in a new situation?

C. Give your opinion.

1. Do you think the teacher treated Yuan in the right way? Why or why not?

2. Were you surprised when Yuan was angry and sad for a few days? Why or why not?

3. How would you have felt if Miss White had talked to you that way?

4. Do you think Yuan's uncle gave good advice? Why or why not?

5. Yuan now observes other people before she tries something new. Do you do the same? Are there other ways to avoid problems? What are these other ways?

CULTURE CAPSULE

Children are called by their first names, but adults are often addressed by their last names with a title in front. The title "Mr." (mister) is used for men. The title "Miss" is used for single women. "Mrs." (missus) is used for married women, and "Ms." (miz) is used for single or married women. In school, students usually address their teachers by whichever of these titles is appropriate and their last name (Ms. Fontes). In college, however, teachers are often called by the special title "professor" and their last name (Professor Dresser). Political figures are also addressed with special titles (Senator Wong, Mayor Garey), as are doctors (Doctor Diaz).

Cultural Exchange

A. *Fill in the chart below and then share your answers with your classmates. Compare your forms of address with the way Americans address each other.*

How Do People Address . . .	Your Country	United States
A mother?		
A father?		
A grandfather?		
A sales clerk?		
A spouse?		
A mother-in-law?		
A boss?		
A college professor?		
A physician?		
A friend?		

spouse—a person's husband or wife

B. *Discuss these questions with your classmates.*

1. In your culture, how are you addressed in a formal situation?

2. In your culture, how are you addressed by close friends?

3. Has any American addressed you in a way that surprised you? Describe what happened.

4. Do you think forms of address are more formal in the United States or in your culture?

5. In your culture, does your family name come first (Disney Walt)? or does your family name come last (Walt Disney)?

6. In your culture, does your name include both your mother's and your father's family name?

7. In your culture, when a woman gets married does she take her husband's name?

8. What are some popular names in your culture?

9. What American names do you like?

Expansion

Work in small groups. Practice using forms of address and titles.

1. Take three index cards and make business cards by writing your name on each of them in three different ways.

   a. On the first card print only your first and last name.

   b. On the second card add either Mr., Miss, Ms., or Mrs. in front of your name.

   c. On the third card give yourself a title before your name—for example, Doctor, Professor, Senator, Mayor, Governor, President, Vice President. Or put a title after your name. You can use Manager, Editor, Attorney-at-Law, Ph.D., D.D.S., or anything else you can think of. Note that when you use a title afterward, you need to add a comma after your name—for example, Betty Woolf, Publisher.

2. Now introduce yourself to a classmate and hand that person your card. You can say these words. "Hello, my name is _____. May I give you my card?" Then have the other person give you one of his or her cards while that person introduces himself or herself to you.

3. When everyone has had a chance to exchange cards, discuss the following questions:

   a. How do you feel when you use just your first and last name?

   b. How do you feel when you have Mr. or Mrs. in front of your name?

   c. How do you feel when you have a professional title?

Role Play

Work in pairs. Choose one of the following situations and role-play it for your classmates. Before you role-play, write the conversation.

Situation 1: Role-play "What Should I Call You?" on pages 64 and 65. Begin your role play when Yuan calls Miss White "teacher," but change what happens next. Have Yuan ask Miss White why she is upset. Have Yuan and Miss White solve their cultural differences.

Use these questions to help you write the conversation:

☐ Does Miss White think Yuan is trying to be disrespectful? How does she react when Yuan asks why she is upset? Does her reaction change when Yuan explains the Chinese custom to her?

☐ How does Yuan, without knowing much English, manage to ask Miss White what the problem is? How does she feel when she finds out that according to American customs she was being disrespectful? How does Yuan then convince Miss White that her mistake was based on a cultural difference?

> Student A=Yuan
> Student B=Miss White

After you role-play, discuss these questions with your classmates:

☐ Did Yuan feel guilty about her mistake? Did Miss White feel guilty about her treatment of Yuan? Did their feelings change during the discussion?

☐ What did Miss White learn from this experience? What did Yuan learn?

Situation 2: Jayasri is from India, and in her ESL class she is introduced to Peter, who misunderstands her name and keeps calling her "J.C." She doesn't like being called J.C., but she is hesitant to correct Peter because he is having such a difficult time learning English. How can she teach him to say her name right without his feeling self-conscious and embarrassed?

Use these questions to help you write the conversation:

☐ How can Jayasri correct Peter? How can she avoid losing his friendship?

☐ Does Peter understand Jayasri's discomfort at being called the wrong name?

> Student A=Jayasri
> Student B=Peter

After you role-play, discuss these questions with your classmates:

☐ Was Peter angry or embarrassed?

☐ Would it have been better if Jayasri had not said anything and had let Peter find out on his own?

☐ Did Jayasri hurt Peter's feelings or did she say the right things?

Follow-Up

A. *Give a brief oral or written report. Tell about your own name. When you do, consider including the following details:*

How was your name chosen?

Who chose it?

Were you named after anyone special?

What is the meaning of your name?

What is the history of your name?

Do you like your name?

Would you like to have someone named after you?

If you could change your name, would you? If so, what would you change it to?

B. *Ms. is a choice of title that either single or married women can use. Interview five Americans and ask them how they feel about single women or married women choosing to use Ms. in front of their names instead of Miss or Mrs. Bring their answers to class and compare them with your classmates' answers.*

U n i t 10
Body Language

❓ Do you know...

1. Do Americans usually look other people directly in the eye or avoid eye contact?

2. What are some gestures you have seen that are commonly used?

An Eye for an Eye

Read the story.

My name is Lorena. I was born in Mexico and came to the United States when I was two. According to Mexican culture, when spoken to by an adult, children show respect by bowing their heads and not looking the adult directly in the eye. This way of showing respect caused me a problem when I went to school.

It was a sunny September morning, my first day at my new private school. The only person I knew was Tina, a girl from my Sunday school, and we sat next to each other and talked. The whole class was talking and giggling; everyone was happy to see old friends again.

Mrs. Georges asked us to be quiet. Then she passed out papers with addition and subtraction problems. Almost immediately, Tina asked me, "What did you get for number four?" I started to tell her, but Mrs. Georges called out, "Lorena, turn around and be quiet!" Just then, the school secretary came into the room with a message for Mrs. Georges. While they were busy speaking, Tina asked me another question. I turned to tell her to stop. Mrs. Georges must have seen me. She called out, "Lorena, come up here right now!"

My hands got moist. My heart beat fast. I took slow, short steps up to Mrs. Georges's desk. In a whisper I said, "Yes, Mrs. Georges?" I looked down at the floor. Mrs. Georges asked, "What were you doing?" I kept my head down and didn't say anything. Her voice got louder. "What were you doing?"

The next thing I knew, Mrs. Georges grabbed my arm tightly. "Look at me when I speak to you!" she said, and she made me look at her. I was scared because I had never before looked into the face of an adult who was speaking to me—not even my parents or grandparents.

For the rest of the day I felt very upset, and when I got home, I told my parents what happened. The next day, my mom went to school with me. We met with Mrs. Georges and explained that in our culture it was

giggling—Laughing in a silly or uncontrolled manner

moist—Slightly wet or damp

grabbed—Seized or grasped with a sudden, rough movement

disrespectful to look an older person in the eye. Mrs. Georges explained that in American culture it was disrespectful *not* to look someone in the eye. When I understood, I told Mrs. Georges that I was sorry. She said she was sorry too, and then she gave me a great big hug.

As a result of this experience I always try to look at anyone who is speaking. I'm a part of America because I live here. I have had to adapt, and now I tell my own child to look at me when I speak to her. I do not want her to experience what I did. That day in school, Mrs. Georges and I learned something about each other's culture. We learned the hard way, but it helped us both.

adapt—Change to fit into a new situation

Comprehension

A. *Tell whether these sentences are true or false.*

1. In Mexico, children show respect for adults by looking them in the eye.

2. On her first day at her new school, Lorena did not know anyone in her classroom.

3. Lorena wanted Tina to give her an answer to a math problem.

4. Mrs. Georges got angry when she saw Lorena turning around to talk to Tina.

5. Lorena became scared when Mrs. Georges called her up to the desk.

6. Lorena had never before looked an adult in the eye while they were speaking.

7. Mrs. Georges apologized when she found out why Lorena would not look her in the eye.

B. *Answer these questions.*

1. What was Lorena taught to do when speaking to adults?

2. How did Lorena know Tina?

3. Why was Lorena about to talk to Tina?

4. How did Lorena feel when Mrs. Georges called her to the desk?

5. Why did Mrs. Georges become really angry and grab Lorena's arm?

6. What happened the next day?

C. Give your opinion.

1. What kind of a person was Tina? Why do you think so?

2. How do you think Lorena felt about Tina after this incident? Why?

3. Do you think Mrs. Georges was a mean or a nice teacher? Explain.

4. Why do you think Americans consider it disrespectful not to look a person in the eye?

5. Were you ever called up to the desk by an angry teacher or did an angry teacher ever ask to see you after class? What happened?

CULTURE CAPSULE

We communicate not only with words but also with "body language" such as facial expressions, gestures, and movements. Like words, body language differs from culture to culture. In some cultures, for example, looking someone in the eye is disrespectful, but in the United States it is a way of showing you are being honest and truthful.

Gestures are the easiest part of body language to describe and learn. Some gestures are as common as words. Moving your head up and down means yes. Moving your head from side to side means no. Lifting your shoulders up and down means you don't know. You can say hello or goodbye by waving your hand up and down or from side to side.

Making a fist with the thumb extended downward is a sign of disapproval, called "thumbs down." Making a fist with the thumb extended upward is a sign of approval, "thumbs up." Another sign that means everything is all right, or "A-OK," is when the index finger joins the thumb to look like a big O.

facial expression—Eye, mouth, or nose movements that communicate a certain meaning

gestures—Movement, usually of the hands, to express a certain meaning

fist—The hand when tightly closed, with the fingers bent into the palm

Cultural Exchange

A. *Fill in the chart below and then share your answers with your classmates. Draw the answers if you can. If not, describe in words.*

What Gestures Do People Make for...	Your Country	United States
Crazy?		
Be quiet?		
Goodbye?		
Go away?		
Come here?		
Yes?		
No?		
Stop?		
Wishing for luck?		
Delicious (food)?		
Everything is fine?		
I don't know?		

B. *Discuss these questions with your classmates.*

1. In your country, what does a smile mean? When is it used? When is it never used?

2. Do you think that in your country gestures are used more often than in the United States, less often, or about as often?

3. In your country, do people use their hands while speaking more often than Americans do?

4. Are some gestures the same in your country and the United States? Which ones? Do some gestures look the same but have different meanings?

5. Are there some gestures from your country that you still find yourself using in the United States? Which ones?

6. Are there some American gestures that you use often? Which ones?

7. Are there any American gestures that you originally had trouble understanding? Which ones?

8. Can you think of any gestures from your culture for which there does not seem to be an American gesture with the same meaning?

9. Can you think of any facial expressions or other kinds of body language besides gestures that are used differently in your country and the United States? What are they?

Expansion

To increase your awareness of how people use body language, make observations outside the classroom.

1. Observe two or three different conversations. If possible, observe conversations involving men and women, Americans and people from other countries, and/or older and younger people. Pay attention to people's body language. You might want to take notes. Try to notice the following:

   What gestures do people use?

   What other examples of body language do people use?

   How far apart do people stand while talking?

   Do people wait for the other person to finish talking or do they interrupt each other? Do people do about the same amount of talking?

   How much eye contact do people make?

2. Compare your observations with observations made by your classmates. Were there differences in body language between men and women? Between Americans and people from other countries? Between older and younger people? If so, what were these differences?

 *Role Play*

Work in groups of three. Choose one of the following situations and role-play it for your classmates. Before you role-play, write the conversation.

Situation 1: Role-play "An Eye for an Eye" on pages 71 and 72. Begin your role play when Mrs. Georges calls Lorena to her desk.

Continued on the following page

Use these questions to help you write the conversation:

☐ Does Mrs. Georges think that Lorena was cheating? Why does she think Lorena won't look at her?

☐ Is Lorena afraid to tell her mother that she got into trouble? How does she expect her mother to respond? Is she worried that she might get into trouble with Mrs. Georges because Lorena told her mother what happened?

☐ Is Lorena's mother angry with Mrs. Georges for upsetting her daughter? Is she angry with Lorena for getting into trouble?

> Student A=Lorena
> Student B=Lorena's mother
> Student C=Mrs. Georges

After you role-play, discuss these questions with your classmates:

☐ Did Mrs. Georges's attitude toward Lorena change? If so, how?

☐ Was it a good idea for Lorena's mother to go into school? Why or why not?

☐ Will Mrs. Georges change her classroom behavior in any way? Explain.

> **Situation 2:** Mr. Nick, an inexperienced ESL teacher, wants to take his class of new Vietnamese students on a tour of the Learning Resources Center. He stands in front of his students, extends his arm, and with his palm facing upward, moves his fingers back and forth as he announces, "Please come with me." No one moves from his or her seat. Mr. Nick repeats his request, speaking in a louder voice and making the same gesture with his hand. Still no one moves from his or her seat. What Mr. Nick does not know is that the gesture he made was an insult to the Vietnamese students—a gesture used only to call a dog or someone who is of low status.
>
> Mr. Nick is confused and becomes impatient. One more time he asks the students to come with him. Nothing happens. How is the problem finally solved? Write the end of the story.

Use these questions to help you write the conversation:

☐ Does Mr. Nick think his students are not very smart or does he think he is doing something wrong when they do not respond? Does he feel angry with his students or angry with himself?

☐ What do the students think when Mr. Nick keeps making this gesture? Do they become angry or puzzled?

☐ Who finally realizes that a misunderstanding must be involved? How does that person help clear up the misunderstanding?

Student A=Mr. Nick

Students B and C=students in Mr. Nick's ESL class

After you role-play, discuss these questions with your classmates:

- ☐ Could the misunderstanding have been cleared up sooner? If so, how?
- ☐ Is Mr. Nick embarrassed when he realizes what was wrong? Is he apologetic to his students?
- ☐ Are the students embarrassed? Are they apologetic to Mr. Nick?
- ☐ Did Mr. Nick and his students learn anything from this incident? Do you think that in the future they will be better able to avoid misunderstandings? Explain.

Follow-Up

A. Give a brief oral or written report. Give an explanation of a gesture used in your own culture. In your report, consider including some of the following details:

Describe the gesture.

What is its meaning?

When is it used? (when a person is angry? happy? sad? afraid?)

When did you first see it used?

Is it used more by men or by women? By children or by adults?

Do you use it often? Why or why not?

Is there an American gesture that has a similar meaning?

B. On a sheet of paper illustrate a gesture from either your own culture or from American culture. Make the drawing large enough so the gesture can easily be seen. Ask your classmates if they know what it means. Ask your teacher to display the drawings, and compare the gestures you and your classmates have drawn.

Touching in Public

? Do you know...

1. Is it acceptable for a male and female to hug or kiss in public?

2. Is it acceptable to walk in public holding hands with someone of the same sex?

I Want to Hold Your Hand

Read the story.

My name is May, and I came from Taiwan. Back there best friends always walk hand in hand, because holding hands is our way of showing friendship. Now that I have been here for several years, I know that friends of the same sex, and even mothers and daughters, seldom go hand in hand, but I didn't know that when I first came to America.

My first year in the United States, I met a girl who had been my classmate in Taiwan. We were excited that we had met again on the other side of the earth, and of course we became best friends. No one really knew about us being best friends because we weren't in the same class. Then one day we were walking hand in hand down the street to get some ice cream. A classmate saw us and seemed very surprised to see us like that. She told us that in the United States, female friends usually don't walk hand in hand or else people will think they are homosexuals. After that, we never went hand in hand in public, but only when we were in our own houses or among Chinese people.

A few months later, my cousin visited me from Taiwan. She immediately noticed that I didn't walk hand in hand with her. She felt sad because she thought I didn't like her as I used to. I tried to explain, but she didn't understand. Finally, a few years later, I went back there for summer vacation. When I went out with my family or old friends shopping, to movies, or anywhere else, I walked hand in hand with them. My cousin was so happy that I liked her again. I told her that I always liked her and that I will explain everything to her when she grows up more. After all, it is hard for a person to understand or accept that other places have different cultures if he or she has never lived in a different place.

homosexuals—Persons who are sexually attracted to the same sex

Comprehension

A. *Tell whether these sentences are true or false.*

1. In Taiwan best friends always walk hand in hand.

2. In the United States best friends always walk hand in hand.

3. May still holds hands with her best friend in her own home.

4. When May would not hold her cousin's hand, the cousin thought May did not like her anymore.

5. May continued the custom of not holding hands when she visited Taiwan.

6. May's cousin is still angry with her.

7. May is able to use Chinese customs in Taiwan and switch to American customs in the United States.

B. *Answer these questions.*

1. In Taiwan how do two persons of the same sex show their friendship?

2. In the United States if two persons of the same sex walk hand in hand what might people think?

3. How did May find out about the American custom of not holding hands?

4. What did the cousin think when May did not walk hand in hand with her?

5. What did the cousin think when May returned to Taiwan and held hands with her again?

6. According to May, why was it hard for her cousin to accept cultural differences?

C. *Give your opinion.*

1. Do you think it was a good idea that May's friend explained the custom of two girls not holding hands? Why or why not?

2. Do you think you would be able to explain something like this to another classmate who was new to this culture? Why or why not?

3. Do you agree with May that it is hard for a person to understand cultural differences if that person has never lived in a different place? Explain your answer.

CULTURE CAPSULE

In the United States, unlike some cultures, a boyfriend and girlfriend can walk down the street holding hands or with their arms around each other. They may even kiss in public and people usually won't mind. A husband and wife can also hold hands or kiss in public. On the other hand, although in many cultures friends walk hand in hand or with their arms around each other, friends in America rarely show affection in these ways.

Cultural Exchange

Discuss these questions with your classmates.

1. In your culture, how do close friends of the same sex express affection when in public? Are the customs for male friends different from those for female friends? Are these ways of expressing affection acceptable in American culture?

2. How would close friends of the opposite sex—who are not, however, girlfriend and boyfriend—express affection when in public in your culture?

3. How would family members express affection when in public in your culture?

4. In your culture, are customs for a husband and wife expressing affection in public different from those for boyfriend and girlfriend? If so, in what ways?

5. What has surprised you about American customs of touching and displaying affection in public?

6. In general, do people who are romantically involved display affection in public more openly in your culture or in American culture? In general, do people who are close friends display affection in public more openly in your culture or in American culture?

Expansion

Work with a partner. Read the situations and decide which is the best answer for each question. Then compare your answers with your classmates' answers.

1. A husband and wife are out walking. They stop and give each other a hug and a kiss on the lips. What will people think?

   a. It is a sign of bad taste.

   b. It is a sign that they love each other.

   c. It is a sign that the husband disrespects his wife.

2. An unmarried man and woman are on a first date. They are waiting in line for a movie and the man pats the woman's behind. What will people think?

   a. The woman should be offended.

   b. She should slap his face.

   c. It is acceptable.

3. At a family wedding a married man asks his unmarried sister-in-law to dance. What will people think?

   a. He disrespects his wife.

   b. It is acceptable.

   c. It is not acceptable.

4. A man and woman in their late seventies are sitting on a park bench. The man gives the woman a passionate kiss. What will people think?

   a. People will smile.

   b. People will be disgusted.

   c. The man and woman should be ashamed.

5. A married man meets in a restaurant a woman friend who is also married. They give each other a kiss on the cheek. What will people think?

   a. They have low morals.

   b. It is acceptable.

   c. Their husband and wife will be angry.

6. A twelve-year-old boy and girl are kissing and walking with their arms around each other. What will people think?

   a. The girl will be considered a "bad" girl.

   b. It is acceptable.

   c. Their parents will not approve.

 # Role Play

Work in groups of three. Choose one of the following situations and role-play it for your classmates. Before you role-play, write the conversation.

Situation 1: Role-play "I Want to Hold Your Hand" on page 79. Begin your role play when May and her friend are going to get ice cream. May's classmate comes by and sees them holding hands.

Use these questions to help you write the conversation:

☐ How do May and her friend feel as they go to get ice cream?

☐ What are they talking about?

☐ How does the classmate react when he or she sees the two friends holding hands? How does the classmate feel about telling them the difference in customs? How does the classmate go about telling them?

☐ How do May and her friend react to what the classmate says?

☐ How do they feel toward the classmate?

> Student A=May
> Student B=May's friend
> Student C=the classmate

After you role-play, discuss these questions with your classmates:

☐ Did the classmate behave in a friendly way? Did he or she try not to make May and her friend feel embarrassed?

☐ Did May and her friend feel grateful that the classmate explained the difference in customs to them?

☐ Do you think May and her friend will ever hold hands again?

☐ What would you have done if you were May? What would you have done if you were the classmate?

Continued on the following page

Situation 2: A father sees his daughter, Madge, holding hands with a boy. He is horrified because in his culture it is considered immoral if a girl holds a boy's hand before they are married. He runs over to his daughter, yelling at her and threatening to punish her. Madge's mother tries to help her daughter by explaining to her husband that American customs are different.

Use these questions to help you write the conversation:

☐ How does Madge feel at her father's outburst? Does she feel guilty, embarrassed, or angry?

☐ Does the father resent the mother for defending the daughter? Does he remain convinced that he is right or does his wife make him change his mind?

☐ How does the mother feel about the situation? Is she convinced that her husband is wrong? Or does she feel torn between sympathy for her daughter and loyalty to her husband and native culture?

Student A=Madge
Student B=Madge's father
Student C=Madge's mother

After you role-play, discuss these questions with your classmates:

☐ Was Madge's mother angry at her husband? Was she angry at Madge?

☐ Did the father's feelings change at all when his wife spoke to him?

☐ Do you think Madge will be able to see her boyfriend anymore? If so, do you think they will still hold hands?

Follow-Up

A. *Give a brief oral or written report. Choose number 1 or 2.*

1. Tell about a time when someone else's public behavior made you feel uncomfortable.

2. Tell about a time when your own public behavior was very different from the behavior of those around you.

In your report, consider including some of the following details:

When did the incident take place?

Where were you living at the time?

Who was involved?

What was their relationship to each other?

What was the behavior that was different or that caused you to be uncomfortable?

What did the behavior mean to you?

How did you react?

How did others react?

As a result of this incident, did anyone change his or her behavior or attitudes?

B. *You are a writer for a magazine in your country. Your assignment is to write an article describing American attitudes about touching in public and other public behavior. In the article, compare American customs with those in your country.*

UNIT 12

Dating

Do you know...

1. At what age do young people in the United States begin dating?

2. If a couple is dating, does this mean that they plan to get married?

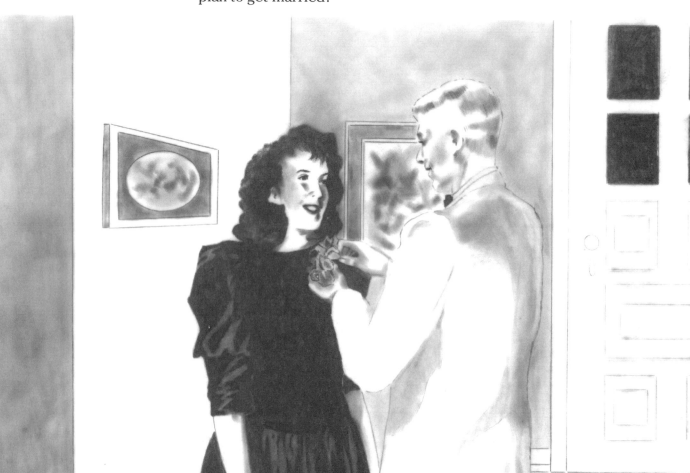

Breaking Up

Read the story.

I am a Chinese girl from Vietnam, and my name is Nancy. My parents, who are very strict, did not let me date until I was eighteen. My first boyfriend was an American guy named Ian. Although my parents were opposed to my seeing him, they learned to accept it because they wanted me to be happy. One day I invited Ian over to my house for dinner so that my parents could meet him. Unfortunately, that invitation led to the end of my relationship with Ian.

According to Chinese custom, the guy a girl is dating is expected to be her future husband. I have been exposed to the American concept that girls can date any guy they want and not have to worry about making commitments. Since my parents are very old-fashioned, we sometimes had arguments about dating. Because of these arguments, I should have realized what my parents would do when Ian came to my house. But I didn't. And Ian only expected to have a nice relaxing dinner with my family.

This "relaxing" dinner became a disastrous dinner when my parents, especially my mom, started asking Ian questions. And I was the one who had to translate these questions. They asked him what his future goals were, what his parents' occupations were, how many brothers and sisters he had, and even what his educational and financial background was. I was shocked that my parents actually asked those questions. Ian was more than shocked—he was obviously stunned. Fortunately, he was very polite and respectful to my parents and suffered through the night. When it was time for Ian to go home, I could tell from the expression on his face that he was glad to be going.

Obviously, Ian noticed that my parents were expecting him to be my future husband. But Ian is an American guy and American guys tend to date a lot before they are ready to settle down. He told me that it was the first time he had ever gone to a girlfriend's house for dinner where he had to answer so many questions

dating—Going out socially with someone of the opposite sex

breaking up—Ending a dating relationship

to be exposed—To learn about

commitments—Promises to be with one person only

stunned—Shocked or surprised

tend to—To be likely to behave in a certain way

about himself and his family. We decided that, because of our different cultural backgrounds, we would just be friends from then on. I believe we made the right decision.

Comprehension

A. Tell whether these sentences are true or false.

1. Nancy's parents were opposed to her dating Ian but learned to accept it.

2. Nancy's parents learned to accept the American concept that a girl can date without making a commitment to marry.

3. Ian knew when he started dating Nancy that he was expected to marry her.

4. The dinner table conversation was all in English.

5. Both Nancy and Ian had a good time.

6. Ian was rude to Nancy's parents.

7. Nancy and Ian are now engaged.

B. Answer these questions.

1. According to Chinese tradition, what does it mean when a girl and a boy are dating?

2. Why did Nancy's parents let her date Ian even though they were opposed to it?

3. What kinds of questions did Nancy's mom ask Ian?

4. How did Nancy react to these questions?

5. How did Ian react to these questions?

6. What happened to Nancy and Ian's relationship?

C. Give your opinion.

1. Do you think Nancy's parents made the right decision to allow her to date someone from another culture? Why or why not?

2. Why do you think Nancy did not try to stop her mother from questioning Ian?

3. Do you think Ian behaved properly at the table? Is there anything he could have done differently to improve the situation?

4. If you had been Nancy, what would you have done to ease the tension at the dinner table?

5. Do you think Nancy and Ian made the right decision to just be friends? Explain your answer.

CULTURE CAPSULE

Some boys and girls may start dating, or "going out," as early as thirteen or fourteen years old. That means they will go somewhere alone or with other friends without any adults along. Later, when they can drive (about sixteen or seventeen), it is acceptable for a boy and a girl to go out together in a car. Dating does not mean that the boy and girl will get married. On the contrary, people think it is a good idea for young adults to go out with different members of the opposite sex. That way they will meet dfifferent kinds of people and learn what kind of person they really want to marry.

Some couples who are in their twenties or older may share an apartment and "live together" before they get married. They think this helps to see whether a marriage might work. But still many parents are opposed to young people living together before marriage.

Cultural  Exchange

A. Fill in the chart below and then share your answers with your classmates.

When it Comes to Dating . . .	Your Country	United States
Can an unmarried male and female go out alone together? Beginning at what age?		
Can a male visit a female's home without their being engaged?		
Can a woman date someone other than the man she will marry?		
Must parents approve of their daughter's date?		
How do young adults find marriage partners? (friends? family? dating services? advertisements? other?)		
What is the usual age difference for an engaged couple?		
What is a typical age at which women marry? What is a typical age for men?		

B. *Discuss these questions with your classmates.*

1. In your country, what happens when a person wants to date someone from a different culture? Does this cause problems or is it acceptable? Explain.

2. In your country, do people ever go on blind dates?

3. In your country, what would be a typical date for a couple in their twenties? (going out to eat? dancing? movie? walking? other?)

4. How would a typical date in your country be similar to a typical date in the United States? How would it differ?

blind date—going out with someone you have never met before

5. What part of American dating customs do you like?

6. What part of American dating customs do you not like?

Expansion

Here is a sample letter:

Many American newspapers have advice columns that answer letters from people asking for advice on love problems or other problems. With a partner, write a letter asking for advice about a problem relating to life in American culture. Switch letters with another pair of students. Write each other a letter giving advice. Share these problems and solutions with the whole class. You can choose a problem from the list on page 91, adding more information, or you can make up your own problem.

```
Dear Broken Hearts Club:

I am a twenty-five-year-old single woman who works in a bank.
I am very happy with my job. I like going out on weekends with
my co-workers. We go shopping, to the movies, and eat out. My
problem is that I am the only one of my brothers and sisters
who is not married. My parents are very unhappy about this.
They believe that all women should get married and have
children, but I am not interested. I would rather just have
a career. And now the bank is offering me a promotion.

My parents are against this. They want me to marry a friend
of theirs—an older businessman. He would like that too, but I
just don't care for him at all. My parents are pressuring me
into a marriage with this man and I am torn between pleasing
my parents and pleasing myself. What should I do?
```

Here are some other problems:

Dear Broken Hearts Club:

1. My boyfriend and I want to get married but my family hates his long hair.

2. I don't know how to meet young women even though I am handsome.

3. Men are just interested in me for my looks; they don't take me seriously as a person.

4. I love my boyfriend, but I don't know how to tell him he needs to take showers more often.

5. I have fallen in love with the man engaged to my sister and I think he loves me too.

6. My wife would rather spend time with her friends than with me.

7. My girlfriend is wonderful but I've heard that she flirts with other guys behind my back.

8. I love my girlfriend but she has a three-year-old son who she brings on all our dates.

9. My boyfriend has a bad temper and when we go out I get embarrassed by how he's always yelling at waiters, salespeople, and everyone else.

10. I'm dating a woman from another culture, and when her family gets together they don't speak my language.

Role Play

Work in groups of three. Choose one of the following situations and then role-play it for your classmates. Before you role-play, write the conversation.

Situation 1: Role-play "Breaking Up" on pages 87 and 88. Begin your role play at the table when Nancy's mom questions Ian.

Use these questions to help you write the conversation:

☐ Is Nancy embarrassed or angry with her mom? Does she feel guilty about putting Ian into this situation?

☐ Is the mom confused by the young man's surprise? Is she angry with her daughter for picking a non-Chinese boyfriend?

☐ Is Ian understanding of Nancy's problem or is he angry with her for putting him into this situation?

Continued on the following page

> Student A=Nancy
> Student B=Nancy's mom
> Student C=Ian

After you role-play, discuss these questions with your classmates:

☐ How did Nancy feel about her mother?

☐ How did Nancy feel about Ian?

☐ Was Ian relieved to be out of the relationship?

☐ Was the mother sorry about the evening or happy that her daughter was finished with Ian?

> **Situation 2:** Angela met Fernando in high school and he really liked her, so one afternoon he came over to her house and asked to watch television with her. Angela wanted to say yes, but her mother said that according to their culture it was disrespectful to have a boy in the house before marriage. They could only visit out on the patio.

Use these questions to help you write the conversation:

☐ Is Angela sympathetic to her mother's belief or is she embarrassed?

☐ Is Angela's mother angry with her or with Fernando?

☐ Is Fernando shocked, angry, uncomfortable, or surprised?

☐ What do Angela and Fernando do about the situation?

> Student A=Angela
> Student B=Angela's mother
> Student C=Fernando

After you role-play, discuss these questions with your classmates:

☐ How did Angela react to her mother's ideas?

☐ Was the mother convinced she was right?

☐ Does Fernando still like Angela? How will this incident affect Fernando and Angela's friendship?

Follow-Up

A. *Give a brief oral or written report. Tell about the dating customs in your culture. In your report, consider including some of the following details:*

How old are young men and women when they begin to date?

Can you date a variety of people or only your future husband/wife?

What are some ways you can meet people to date?

Where do you go on dates?

Do other people accompany you?

Must you be home by a certain hour?

Does the man pay for all expenses?

Does the man ever give gifts to the woman? Does the woman ever give gifts to the man? What kinds of gifts are given?

What are the advantages and disadvantages of your dating customs compared with American dating customs?

B. *In the United States, some people find a boyfriend or girlfriend by advertising in newspapers or magazines. Sometimes they may even go to a computerized dating service.*

Pretend that you are unmarried and are looking for someone to date and eventually marry. Fill in the blanks of the questionnaire to help you find the man or woman of your dreams.

I am looking for the _____ of my dreams. _____ should be
   (man or woman)   (He or she)
about _____ tall and weigh about_____. This person should
         (height)   (weight)
have _____ hair and _____ eyes and I want someone who
         (color)   (color)
likes to _____ and is also interested in _____.
       (hobby or sport)   (another interest)
I hope this person likes to listen to _____ music and likes to eat
                                      (favorite music)
_____ because these are my favorites. I hope I can find my ideal mate
   (favorite food)
who has a _____ personality and one who also
              (describe)

_____.
                              (finish on your own)

U N I T 13

Weddings

? Do you know...

1. What is the traditional color for wedding gowns?

2. What do the maid of honor and the best man do at a wedding?

Lady in Red

Read the story.

I'm from China, and my name is Su. The problem I will tell about began one day when I was sitting with friends at lunchtime talking and laughing. My friend Jan told the rest of us that we were invited to her sister's wedding. I was very excited because I had never been to an American wedding. Her sister's wedding was going to be held the following week.

When school was over, I rushed home so excited that I forgot to take my algebra book. I was thinking of what to wear to the wedding. I thought of wearing black and white but then decided that would not be appropriate for a wedding. Well, I sat in my room thinking for hours and still I couldn't come up with anything. Then, looking around my room, I noticed something red and thought, why not wear all red to the wedding?

I asked my mother her opinion and she told me that red would be a good color, that in China the color red was for good luck. The next day she went shopping with me. We couldn't find anything for several hours. Finally, I found a red suit that I thought was fabulous. It was made out of silk; the pants were very baggy, and the blouse was like a jacket with see-through sleeves. Next, I went to buy a pair of shoes. I bought a white pair with cute red bows on the front.

The day of the wedding my friends picked me up so that we could go together to Jan's house. I was the only one who was wearing red. When we got to Jan's house, she greeted us and gave me this funny look, which I didn't like. She seemed mad, but I didn't know why. When she introduced us to her family, her family also gave me this funny look I didn't like. After that, Jan and her family never spoke to me once the whole day. I wanted to cry because everyone kept looking at me like I had done something wrong.

Finally, the wedding was over. I got home and told my mom what happened. The next day, Jan called me and said we couldn't be friends anymore, but she

---

didn't give me a reason. Later on, one of my friends told me that in Jan's religion the color red represents the devil. To Jan and her family my red dress was disrespectful and a sign of bad luck. They thought that by wearing red I was putting the wedding couple in danger. My friend also told me that at most American weddings the red suit would not have been a problem at all. I found all this confusing, but at least I finally understood what had happened.

In conclusion, I think that people shouldn't stop being friends or get angry at other people if they do something wrong just because of a cultural misunderstanding. I think people should talk things over before ending their friendship.

Comprehension

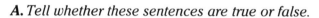

A. *Tell whether these sentences are true or false.*

1. Su's friend Jan was getting married.

2. Su had been to other American weddings.

3. Su did not think she should wear black and white to a wedding.

4. Su's mom did not think she should wear red.

5. Su spent a lot of time shopping for her outfit.

6. Jan was happy to see Su when she arrived at the wedding.

7. Because of their religious beliefs, the family of the bride was offended by Su's clothes.

8. After the wedding Jan explained to Su why they could not be friends anymore.

B. *Answer these questions.*

1. Why did Su forget to bring her algebra book home?

2. What did Su's mother say about wearing red?

3. What did Su buy to wear to the wedding?

4. How did Jan and her family respond to Su at the wedding?

5. How did this make Su feel?

6. Why was the family offended?

C. *Give your opinion.*

1. Do you think that Jan should have told people not to wear red? Why or why not?

2. Do you think Jan's family should have been more understanding about Su's mistake?

3. How do you think the bride and groom felt when they saw Su?

4. Do you think Jan should have explained to Su why they could not be friends? Why or why not?

5. Do you think there is some way that this incident could have turned out to be more positive? Explain your answer.

CULTURE CAPSULE

At a traditional wedding, the bride wears a long, fancy white dress and a veil and the groom wears a tuxedo. Friends and family of the bride and groom take part in the ceremony. The bride chooses a maid of honor to help her during the ceremony and bridesmaids who also walk down the aisle. Generally, the maid of honor and the bridesmaids wear matching dresses. The best man helps the groom during the ceremony. He and the other male assistants, called ushers, all wear tuxedos, or formal suits. Other wedding guests often wear their nicest clothing. There are no rules, though, except that females generally do not wear white, to avoid competing with the bride.

Different ethnic and religious groups have their own customs for weddings, including customs about what to wear. Also, many couples decide not to have traditional weddings, preferring wedding ceremonies that are less formal.

veil—Covering of net or fine cloth for the head or face

maid of honor—The principal bridesmaid who helps the bride

bridesmaids—Women, often unmarried, who help the bride on the day of the marriage ceremony

aisle—A space to walk through or between sections of seats as in a church or theater

tuxedo—A man's formal evening suit, usually black

competing—Trying to look or to do better than someone else

ethnic—Cultural, religious, national, or racial group

Cultural Exchange

A. *Fill in the chart and then share your answers with your classmates.*

At a Wedding . . .	Your Country	United States
What does the bride wear?		
What does the groom wear?		
Who pays for the wedding?		
What kinds of food and beverages are served?		
Is there music and dancing?		
Are there colors that guests should not wear?		

B. *Discuss these questions with your classmates.*

1. In your culture, do the parents of either the bride or the groom give them money? Explain.

2. In your culture, when do friends and relatives give gifts to the bride and groom? What kinds of gifts are given?

3. In your culture, do married women wear a ring? On what finger? Do married men wear a ring? On what finger?

4. In your culture, does the newly married couple go on a brief holiday together following the wedding ceremony? Explain.

5. In your culture, do the newlyweds live on their own or do they live with either the bride's family or the groom's family? If they live on their own, who furnishes the new home?

6. Have you been to any American weddings? Were they similar to weddings in your culture?

7. Does anything about American wedding customs surprise you? Explain.

8. What kind of wedding would you like to have? Or, if you are married, what kind of wedding did you have?

Expansion

To increase your vocabulary about wedding customs, solve this crossword puzzle with words from the list below.

best man	garter	maid of honor	stag
bouquet	gifts	reception	thank-you
bride	groom	rice	trousseau
bridesmaids	honeymoon	ring	ushers
cake	I do	shower	veil
fun			

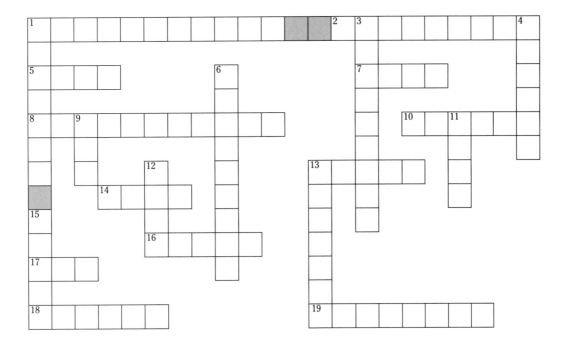

Across

1 Female attendants of the bride
2 Personal items the bride-to-be accumulates before the wedding
5 All-male party given for the groom before the wedding: _____ party
7 Dessert served at all wedding parties
8 Female attendant who stands next to the bride
10 Sometimes worn by the bride around her leg
13 The woman who is getting married
14 Worn over the bride's face before the ceremony
16 The man who is getting married
17 What guests at the wedding party are expected to have
18 Party given for the bride before the wedding: bridal _____
19 Notes written by the bride after receiving wedding gifts: _____ _____ notes

Down

1 Male attendant who hands groom the ring
3 Party given after the wedding ceremony
4 Male attendants at a wedding
6 Holiday the newlyweds take following the wedding
9 Words spoken during the ceremony
11 Thrown at the bride and groom as they leave the place where they were married
12 Placed on the bride's finger
13 Bride throws this to the unmarried women—whoever catches it will be the next one married
15 Given to the bride and groom by friends and family

Role Play

Work in pairs. Choose one of these situations and role-play it for your classmates. Before you role-play, write the conversation.

Situation 1: Role-play "Lady in Red" on pages 95 and 96. Begin your role play when Su arrives at the wedding. After Jan treats her coldly, have Su ask Jan what is wrong and have Jan explain the problem.

Use these questions to help you write the conversation:

☐ Is Su angry, embarrassed, unhappy, or just puzzled?

☐ Is Jan angry? Is she worried that her parents are angry with her for inviting an outsider who spoiled the wedding?

☐ Does Jan realize that Su just made a mistake?

☐ How does Su react to Jan's explanation? How does Jan react now?

Student A=Su
Student B=Jan

After you role-play, discuss these questions with your classmates:

☐ How did Su feel before the talk with Jan? How did Jan feel?

☐ Did the conversation change the way Su felt? Did it change the way Jan felt?

☐ Will Su and Jan continue to be friends or has the friendship probably ended?

Situation 2: A young adult announces to his or her parent that he or she is getting married, and because the couple met in the park they want to get married there, wear blue jeans and T-shirts, and have a wedding picnic. The parent is horrified and insists on a traditional religious wedding ceremony. What kind of wedding do they have?

Use these questions to help you write the conversation:

☐ Why is the parent so upset? Has the parent always wanted a traditional wedding or is the parent just worried about what friends and relatives might think?

☐ Did the child expect the parent to be upset? How would the child feel about not being able to plan his or her own wedding?

☐ What would be the effects on the child agreeing to a traditional wedding?

☐ What would be the effects on the parent agreeing to a wedding in the park?

☐ What happens? How does each person now feel?

> Student A=the son or daughter
> Student B=the father or mother

After you role-play, discuss these questions with your classmates:

☐ How did the person who got his or her own way feel?

☐ Did this person feel convinced he or she was right or did the individual feel a little guilty?

☐ How did the person who did not get his or her own way feel?

☐ Why did this person agree to something he or she did not really want?

☐ Do you agree with the way the parent and child resolved the problem?

☐ Do you think this solution will work or do you think there will be more problems about the wedding?

Follow-Up

A. *Give a brief oral or written report. Choose number 1 or 2.*

1. Describe a wedding ceremony you attended that was from your own cultural tradition.

2. Describe a wedding ceremony you attended that was different from weddings in your own culture.

In your report, consider including some of the following details:

When did this wedding take place?

Where did the wedding take place?

What was the cultural background of the bride and groom?

How was the bride dressed?

Did she have attendants? Who were they? How were they dressed?

How was the groom dressed?

Did he have attendants? Who were they? How were they dressed?

Did the parents of the bride and groom do anything special during the ceremony?

Was there any kind of party after the ceremony? (music? food? dancing?)

Did anything unusual take place? Describe.

Did you have a good time? Why or why not?

B. *With a partner, make a list of household items you think every newly married couple needs. Compare your list with classmates' lists. What items are mentioned most often?*

U N I T 14

Good Luck and Bad Luck

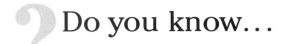 **Do you know…**

1. What do Americans consider to be lucky?
2. What do Americans consider to be unlucky?

Debby's Birthday Present

Read the story.

My name is Debby. I was born in China and lived for many years in Hong Kong. When my family moved to the United States, there were many things that we were not used to. We worked hard to learn and accept the American life-style and culture. Making changes was especially difficult for my grandparents. They believe that Chinese people should follow Chinese customs no matter where they are.

Three years ago I met a girl named Reyna. She is Hispanic-American and has lived in the United States all her life. We became good friends almost right away. She taught me how to eat Mexican food, and I taught her how to use chopsticks. She told me about Mexican culture, and I told her about Chinese celebrations like the celebration of the full moon. On my sixteenth birthday, I invited Reyna to my house to have dinner with my family. My grandmother had made all of my favorite Chinese foods. When Reyna came to the house, she handed me a birthday gift. My family liked Reyna very much. We had a very nice dinner together, and after dinner we decided to open my gifts. Since I was eager to know what Reyna gave me, I opened her gift first. It was a black and white clock.

When my grandparents saw the clock, the expressions on their faces changed instantly. They became very angry and left the living room. Reyna didn't understand what was happening. I explained that getting a clock as a gift is bad luck, and to Chinese people, black and white objects are also bad luck. So, to my grandparents, the gift that Reyna gave me meant double bad luck on my birthday. I also told Reyna that another meaning of a clock is the end of life. After she heard my explanation of the meaning of her gift, she felt very bad. She didn't know what to do.

When Reyna left, my grandparents told me that I should not be her friend anymore, since she had wished me death on my birthday. I tried to explain that American people do not have that belief, but my grandparents wouldn't accept my explanation.

The next day, Reyna came to my house again. My grandparents were very rude to her. She gave me a bright red box and said, "Happy Birthday." I was surprised that she was not angry at the way my grandparents treated her. I opened the red box. Inside was a bright red dress. I tried it on, and it looked great on me. I showed it to my grandparents and told them it was from Reyna. They smiled at me and Reyna and told her they liked it very much.

As a result of this incident, I learned that Reyna was very understanding and a great friend to have. Obviously, Reyna learned never to give clocks or black and white gifts to Chinese people.

rude—Not polite; discourteous

Comprehension

A. Tell whether these sentences are true or false.

1. Debby's grandparents did not want to adapt to American culture.

2. Reyna taught Debby about Mexican culture.

3. As soon as Debby's family saw Reyna, they did not like her.

4. In Chinese culture, a clock can mean death.

5. In Chinese culture, black and white means good luck.

6. Reyna felt bad about what she did.

7. When Reyna brought over the red dress in the red box, Debby was very happy.

8. Debby's grandparents never forgave Reyna.

B. Answer these questions.

1. Why were the grandparents offended when they saw the gift from Reyna?

2. What did the grandparents want Debby to do about her friendship with Reyna?

3. What did Reyna do to try to make up for her cultural mistake?

4. How did the grandparents react to the gift in the red box?

5. What did Debby and Reyna each learn from this experience?

C. Give your opinion.

1. Why do you think it was hard for Debby's grandparents to accept the American life-style and culture?

2. Do you think Debby is close with her grandparents? Explain.

3. Do you think Debby's grandparents should have been kinder about the clock? Why do you think they weren't kinder?

4. Why did Reyna bring over a red dress in a red box?

5. What does this tell you about Reyna? Would you want her for your friend? Why?

CULTURE CAPSULE

Thirteen is thought to be an unlucky number. Most hotels do not have a thirteenth floor or a room number 13 because people might not stay there. Friday the thirteenth is thought to be an unlucky day. Many people do not want to do anything dangerous, like have surgery, on Friday the thirteenth, and some do not even like to leave their houses. Some people believe that bad luck can come if a black cat crosses their path or if they open an umbrella inside the house, walk under a ladder, or break a mirror. There are also many superstitions about good luck. Some people think they will have good luck if they find a four-leaf clover, hang a horseshoe over their door, or wear a rabbit's foot.

superstitions—Beliefs that are not based on reason but are based on magic or old ideas

Cultural Exchange

A. Fill in the chart and then share your answers with your classmates.

According to Superstition, What Are Some . . .	Your Country	United States
Good luck charms to wear or carry? to hang in your home or car?		
Good luck numbers?		
Bad luck numbers?		
Bad luck omens? (black cat? broken mirror? full moon? spilled salt? other?)		
Good luck omens? (falling star? other?)		
Good luck colors?		
Bad luck colors?		

UNIT 14   *Good Luck and Bad Luck*

B. *Discuss these questions with your classmates.*

1. In your culture, are there some things that you would never do because they might bring bad luck? (compliment a baby? open an umbrella inside the house? tell about something good before it happens? other?) Describe.

2. In your culture, is there anything you do to protect yourself from bad luck? (cross yourself? knock on wood? spit three times? cross your fingers? other?) Describe.

3. Are there things from your culture that some family members do, which you do not do because you consider them too superstitious?

4. According to your culture are there any things that you can do to change bad luck to good luck? (sprinkle something around the house? consult a special person? bathe in special oils? other?)

5. Do you find that many American superstitions are the same as superstitions in your country? Are there any American superstitions that have surprised you?

Expansion

Interview at least two people outside of class and ask them if they know anything about the American superstitions listed below. Ask them if they know these superstitions, if they practice or believe them, and if they are from another country, do they have something similar. Bring your answers back to class and compare them with your classmates' answers.

1. If you spill salt, you will have bad luck.

2. If you leave a hat on the bed, you will have bad luck.

3. If you see a falling star, you will have good luck.

4. If you knock on wood, it will keep bad luck from happening.

5. If you blow out all the candles on the birthday cake, you will have good luck.

6. If you see an owl flying or hear it hooting in the daytime, you will have bad luck.

7. If your palm itches, you will receive money.

8. If the groom sees the bride in her wedding dress before the ceremony, it is a sign of bad luck.

9. If a ladybug lands on you, you will have good luck.

10. If you find a coin and pick it up, you will have good luck.

 *Role Play*

Work in groups of three. Choose one of the following situations and role-play it for your classmates. Before you role-play, write the conversation.

Situation 1: Role-play "Debby's Birthday Present" on pages 104 and 105. Begin your role play when Debby opens up the present. Debby's grandmother (or grandfather) sees it and reacts.

Use these questions to help you write the conversation:

☐ How does the grandparent feel when he (she) thinks a stranger wishes death to Debby?

☐ What does Reyna feel—embarrassment? anger?

☐ Does Debby feel torn between loyalty to her family and to her friend? What does Debby, who understands both cultures, do?

> Student A=Debby
> Student B=Reyna
> Student C=the grandparent

After you role-play, discuss these questions with your classmates:

☐ How did Debby handle the misunderstanding? How did Reyna handle it?

☐ How did the grandmother feel toward Reyna in the end?

☐ How will this event affect Reyna's relationship with Debby?

Situation 2: Andrea, an artist, gives a pair of elephant bookends she has made to her friend Kay. When Kay's husband, George, sees the elephants he is horrified because the elephant trunks are down instead instead of up. In his culture, this is a sign of bad luck. He does not want bad luck in their home. George wants Kay to return the elephants to Andrea. Write the ending.

Use these questions to help you write the conversation:

☐ How frightened is George that the elephant trunks mean bad luck? Does he care about not hurting Andrea's feelings or not ruining his wife's friendship with Andrea?

☐ Does Kay feel caught in the middle between George and Andrea? Is she worried about bad luck too? Is she worried about ruining her friendship with Andrea? Is she afraid of her husband's anger?

☐ Will Andrea understand the problem? How offended would she be to have her gift returned?

> Student A=Andrea
> Student B=George
> Student C=Kay

After you role-play, discuss these questions with your classmates:

☐ Was George willing to change his way of thinking? Was Andrea? How did each of the three people behave?

☐ Was Andrea's friendship with Kay ruined?

☐ What do you think of this ending to the story?

Follow-Up

A. *Give a brief oral or written report. Choose number 1 or 2.*

1. Tell about a time when you gave someone a gift that brought an unexpected reaction.

2. Tell about an experience when you had either good or bad luck.

If you choose number 1, consider including some of the following details:

When did this incident occur? Where were you living at the time?

What was the occasion for the gift?

Whom were you giving it to? What was the gift?

What response did you expect? What response did you receive?

How did it affect your relationship with the person?

What did you learn from this experience?

If you choose number 2, consider including some of the following details:

When did this incident occur?

Where were you living at the time?

Did you have good luck or bad luck?

What caused it?

What happened as a result of the good luck or bad luck?

What did you learn from the experience?

Has this bad luck or good luck occurred again since that time?

B. *Using an encyclopedia, work alone or with a partner and look up two of the following words. Write down their meanings and compare your answers with your classmates' answers. What do these words have in common? Which of these things exist in your culture?*

amulet	fortune-telling	oracles
astrology	ghost	Ouija board
dowsing	graphology	palmistry
evil eye	omens	seance

U N I T 15
Parents and Children

? ## Do you know...

1. At what age is it acceptable for children to move out of their parents' home?

2. How are children usually punished?

Respect

Read the story.

My name is Lily, and I was raised in a very conservative family on the island of Fiji, in the South Pacific. At an early age we were taught close family ties and conservative ways. Family members worked together as one unit, and we respected our elders. Upon arriving in the United States, I discovered a very different world, where children speak as they wish to their parents and at times even treat them with disrespect. This different world eventually led to some difficulties between me and my parents.

When I was eighteen, a couple of my friends moved out of their parents' house and into an apartment of their own. They asked me to move in with them. These friends were born in the United States, and their upbringing was less conservative than mine. Their parents considered it perfectly acceptable for them to move out and live independently at eighteen. But when I spoke to my parents, it was clear they did not want me to leave home. My friends couldn't understand this and they kept telling me to move out anyway. I felt caught between my friends and my parents. I felt that my friends were doing something that was socially acceptable and "in with the crowd" and that my parents were being old-fashioned and not behaving as Americans should behave.

For me, after many sleepless nights, my obligation as a daughter overcame my yearning for independence. I realized that my parents' unwillingness for me to move out was because of their love for me. I also realized that if my friends were true friends they would accept my decision. I told them I'd decided to stay with my parents. Some of my friends and I grew apart from each other but most of my friends accepted my decision. They realized that it did not matter whether I lived with my parents, that what really mattered for our friendship was how I was with them. Now, looking back, I feel that an eighteen-year-old is still young enough to make many mistakes, and I feel lucky that I didn't make a mistake.

elders—Older persons

upbringing—Training and education during childhood

obligation—One's duty

yearning—Having strong desire or great longing

Comprehension

A. *Tell whether these sentences are true or false.*

1. Lily grew up in the United States.

2. Lily thinks that American children are sometimes disrespectful to their parents.

3. Lily's friends wanted her to move into an apartment with them.

4. Lily's parents encouraged her to move out.

5. Lily was torn between independence and obedience.

6. Lily decided to move out.

7. Lily now regrets the decision she made.

8. Lily lost some friends as a result of her decision.

B. *Answer these questions.*

1. What did Lily learn when she was growing up in Fiji?

2. What did Lily's friends want her to do?

3. Why was it acceptable for Lily's friends to move out?

4. Why didn't Lily's parents want her to move out?

5. Looking back, what does Lily now realize?

6. What happened to Lily's friendships as a result of her decision?

C. *Give your opinion.*

1. What do you think about the idea of children living on their own at age eighteen?

2. Do you think Lily made the right decision? Explain.

3. What kind of person is Lily? How do you know this?

4. What do you think about the way Lily's friends reacted to her decision? If you were a friend of Lily's would her decision have affected your friendship?

5. Were you ever in a situation where your friends felt one way and your parents felt another way? What did you do?

CULTURE CAPSULE

Generally, American parents want their children to become independent. Therefore, they often encourage their children to make their own decisions, give their own opinions, and get jobs outside the home. It is also generally acceptable for children over eighteen to move out and get their own apartments, especially since eighteen is the usual age for finishing high school and going on to college or getting a full-time job.

American parents may seem to be less strict than parents in some other cultures. But rules and discipline vary a lot from family to family; while some parents are lenient, others are strict.

strict—severe; requiring complete obedience

discipline—training to produce obedience and self-control

lenient—Mild, not severe

Cultural Exchange

A. *Fill in the chart and then share your answers with your classmates.*

In a Typical Family . . .	Your Country	United States
What household chores do children have?		
Are children expected to be "seen but not heard"?		
What are acceptable forms of punishment?		
How do children express respect for parents? (words? obedience? hugs and kisses?)		
Do unmarried sons move out? (unmarried daughters?) At what age?		

B. *Discuss these questions with your classmates.*

1. In your culture, are children encouraged to be independent? Explain. Do you think that the American way of encouraging independence is a good idea? Why or why not?

2. In your culture, are children given an allowance or spending money? Explain. What can they do with it?

3. In your culture, are working children expected to give money to the family? Explain.

4. In your culture, are family matters discussed openly in front of the children?

5. In your culture, if children have problems who do they discuss them with?

6. Do you think that children in American culture are less respectful to their parents than in your culture?

7. Are there any American ways of raising children that you would like to follow? Are there any American ways of raising children that you would never follow?

Expansion

In groups of at least four people, choose one of the parent/child issues listed below. Each group divides into two sides—one agreeing with the child, the other agreeing with the parents. Each side makes a list of reasons why their position on the issue is correct. Then both sides present their reasons to the rest of the class. The other class members can vote to see whether they support the child or the parents.

1. A son wants to quit college for a high-paying job. His parents want him to complete his education.

2. A daughter wants to get married. The parents do not approve of the man she wants to marry because he has no job.

3. A daughter wants to become an airline pilot. Her parents feel this is not the proper job for a woman.

4. The eldest son has been offered an excellent job out of the country. His parents do not want him to leave.

5. A child has musical ability, but is only interested in rock and roll. Her parents object to this music.

Role Play

Work in groups of three. Choose one of the following situations and role-play it for your classmates. Before you role-play, write the conversation.

Situation 1: Role-play "Respect" on page 112. Begin your role play when one of Lily's friends invites her to share an apartment. Have Lily discuss the invitation with her mother.

Use these questions to help you write the conversation:

☐ What does Lily want to do? Is she afraid to say no to her friend? Is she afraid to tell her mother?

☐ Is Lily's mother upset by the invitation? Does she worry about Lily being friends with people who have different values?

☐ What does the friend think when Lily says no? Is she disappointed or angry?

Student A=Lily
Student B=Lily's friend
Student C=Lily's mother

After you role-play, discuss these questions with your classmates:

☐ Did Lily's mother treat her in a way that was fair?

☐ How does Lily feel in the end—disappointed or satisfied?

☐ Do you think Lily's friendship will be affected?

Situation 2: Two teenage friends, Zack and Avi, drive to a party together. It is 11:00 P.M. and Avi wants to leave because he has to be home by 11:30. Zack does not have to be home at any special time and he wants to stay, so he talks Avi into staying until 1:00 A.M. When Avi gets home, his angry father is waiting for him.

Use these questions to help you write the conversation:

☐ How does Avi feel being torn between pleasing his father and his friend?

☐ Is Avi more afraid of losing his friendship with Zack or facing his father's anger and punishment?

☐ Does Zack think Avi is a "baby" because he wants to please his father by being home on time? Does he have more respect for him because he stays?

☐ Is the father angrier at Avi for not obeying or at Zack for talking Avi into staying out late?

☐ Is there any kind of punishment for Avi? Can he still be friends with Zack?

Student A=Avi
Student B=Zack
Student C=Avi's father

After you role-play, discuss these questions with your classmates:

☐ Was it difficult for Zack to convince Avi to stay out late?

☐ In the end, is Avi angry at Zack for getting him into trouble?

☐ How did Zack react when Avi wanted to go home?

☐ How did Zack react when he saw how angry Avi's father was?

☐ Was the father disappointed in Avi?

☐ Do you think that the way the father treated Avi was fair?

Follow-Up

A. Give a brief oral or written report. Choose number 1 or 2.

1. Tell about a time when you did something against your parents' rules.

2. Tell about a time when your child did something against your rules.

In your report, consider including some of the following details:

How long ago did this happen?

Where were you living at the time?

How old was the child?

Continued on the following page

What rule was broken?

What happened afterward?

How did the child feel?

How did the parent feel?

Was there any kind of punishment? Describe.

What did you learn from this experience?

B. *Pretend you are a parent. Your eighteen-year-old has asked your permission to move out of the house into an inexpensive apartment. You child wants to do this because he or she wants to learn how to become more independent, learn how to handle money, and make his or her own decisions.*

Write a letter to your child; try to convince him or her why you think it is a good or bad idea for the child to move out. Give some reasons why you think the way you do.

UNIT 16
The Classroom

? Do you know...

1. Do American teachers generally prefer students to be quiet or to ask questions?

2. How do teachers react when students disagree with them?

School Daze

Read the story.

Call me Henry. I grew up in Vietnam, where we usually don't ask questions or have much contact with the teacher. Rarely will a student raise his hand. From the day I entered kindergarten and all the way through high school, I just listened and took notes in class. Each evening it was my responsibility to memorize the materials that were presented in class that day. There were no discussions, debates, or challenges to the teacher's point of view. The teacher was always right because he was the teacher. He knew the stuff better than me.

When I came to the United States the school system surprised me. My classes were hardly ever quiet. One day we had a discussion on the topic of gun control. Everyone participated in it. The class atmosphere was exciting and fun. The arguing went on until the end of the class, and everyone seemed to enjoy it. To my surprise the teacher encouraged the discussion and listened to what the students had to say. This felt very different to me. The teacher was treating the students like friends, not like in Vietnam where teachers kept their distance from the students. Hearing the discussion, I learned there were many different opinions on the question of gun control. I also learned that a person who is good at communicating can persuade other people to change their points of view.

Thinking back on school days in Vietnam, I realized that I wasn't very good at communicating with people because I hadn't had the practice. I couldn't even express myself clearly about the materials that I learned in Vietnam. Fortunately, during the gun control discussion, the teacher didn't call on me to state my opinion.

From that day I have been working on expressing my thoughts in a clear manner so that people can understand what I mean.

daze—To be in a state of confusion

School Daze—A play on words; the usual expression is "School Days," meaning the time spent in school; by changing *days* to *daze*, it means the confusion caused by being in school

challenges—Objections or questions about the rightness or truthfulness of something

Comprehension

A. *Tell whether these sentences are true or false.*

1. In Vietnam, Henry only listened, took notes, and memorized.
2. In Vietnam, the teacher was always right.
3. Henry was bored in his American classroom.
4. Henry was very surprised by his American classroom.
5. The American teacher was very strict and the students were afraid of him.
6. Henry learned there were different sides to the issue of gun control.
7. Henry prefers the Vietnamese method of education.
8. Henry learned about the importance of good communication skills.

B. *Answer these questions.*

1. What are Vietnamese students supposed to do in class?
2. What surprised Henry about his American classroom?
3. How did the American students respond to the topic of gun control?
4. How did the teacher respond to the noise and differences of opinion?
5. What is Henry trying to do to improve his American classroom abilities?

C. *Give your opinion.*

1. What do you think is a more effective way to learn—memorization or discussion? Explain.
2. Do you think Henry will find it easy or hard to adapt to the American system? Explain.
3. Do you think it is easier or harder to be a teacher in Vietnam (according to the way Henry described) or the United States?
4. Do you approve of the way Henry's teacher dealt with the issue of gun control?

CULTURE CAPSULE

Teachers will not be angry if students disagree. Actually, they like students who speak up in class by asking questions and giving their own ideas. Because they encourage participation, teachers often use small-group discussions that ask for student opinions. Generally, teachers do not require memorization of many facts.

Students are also encouraged to participate in after-school activities like sports teams, orchestra, and leadership classes. It is generally believed that students who have interests beyond getting good grades will have more chances of getting into better colleges and universities.

Cultural Exchange

A. *Fill in the chart and then share your answers with your classmates.*

Concerning School . . .	Your Country	United States
At what age does a child start school?		
How many years are required?		
Is it free? If not, how much does it cost?		
Is physical punishment allowed?		
Do students wear uniforms?		
How much homework is given?		
Is questioning of teachers encouraged?		
Do students raise their hands when they want the teacher to call on them?		
Do students stand when the teacher enters the room?		

B. *Discuss these questions with your classmates.*

1. In your culture, is it all right for a student to copy someone else's work or copy from the book? Explain.

2. In your culture, how is it determined who goes to college?

3. In your culture, do teachers treat students in an informal way or is there a distance between them? Explain.

4. In your culture, what kind of preparation must a teacher have?

5. In your culture, is teaching a highly respected profession? Is teaching a well-paid profession?

6. Have teachers in the United States treated you differently from the way teachers in your own country treated you? Explain.

7. Do you think that teachers in the United States give more or less homework than in your country? Is this good or bad? Why?

8. What has surprised you about going to school in the United States?

Expansion

Work in pairs. One person is an elementary school teacher, Mr. Roberts. The other is a parent of any one of the students listed below. The parent phones Mr. Roberts and asks him to give a progress report on the child. Begin as in the example below. Use the information provided and your imagination to continue the conversation.

MRS. BAKER: *Hello, Mr. Roberts? This is Mrs. Baker, Lino's mother. Can you please tell me how my son is doing?*

MR. ROBERTS: *Mrs. Baker, Lino is doing very well in math, but . . . .*

Name of Student	Behavior	Reading	Math	Social Studies
Melissa Costa	talks too much	B	B+	A
Lino Baker	troublemaker	D	A	C
Corie Espinoza	perfect	A	A	A
Tony Cobb	seems disinterested	D	D	F
Jasmine Choy	obedient	C–	D	C–
Eric Miller	often absent or late	C	C	C

Role Play

Work in groups of three. Choose one of the following situations and role-play it for your classmates. Before you role-play, write the conversation.

Situation 1: Mr. Cappella, a teacher, discovers Brian copying Mark's work during a test. He accuses them of cheating, and they are surprised. They insist that in their culture it is not considered cheating to help a friend. Write the ending.

Use these questions to help you write the conversation:

☐ Is Mr. Cappella surprised that the boys think this is acceptable behavior? Does he think they are just trying to use their background to avoid getting into trouble? Will he accept their explanation?

☐ Do Mark and Brian really believe that Mr. Cappella will accept this cultural-difference excuse? Are they sincere? Or are they only trying to avoid punishment?

Student A=Mr. Cappella
Student B=Mark
Student C=Brian

After you role-play, discuss these questions with your classmates:

☐ Did Brian and Mark seem to be telling the truth?

☐ Do you agree with the way Mr. Cappella handled the situation? If not, what do you think he should have done?

Situation 2: Isa, who is doing poorly in school, gives an expensive purse to the teacher, Mrs. Sterling. The teacher is shocked by the gift and speaks with Isa and her mother. She gives back the gift and tells them that bribery is not acceptable in America. Isa's mother is shocked and offended. In their culture it is common to give expensive gifts to the teacher to show appreciation.

Use these questions to help you write the conversation:

☐ Does Isa feel embarrassed because the teacher rejects the gift?

☐ Does Mrs. Sterling believe the cultural-differences excuse?

☐ Is she angry with Isa and her mother? Or is she sympathetic?

☐ Does Isa's mother feel embarrassed or is she angry that Mrs. Sterling does not accept their cultural differences?

> Student A=Isa
> Student B=Mrs. Sterling
> Student C=Isa's mother

After you role-play, discuss these questions with your classmates:

☐ Did Mrs. Sterling change her view of the situation after talking to Isa and her mother?

☐ Do you agree with the way Mrs. Sterling handled the situation? Do you agree with the way Isa's mother handled the situation?

☐ How do you think Isa and Mrs. Sterling will get along after this episode?

Follow-Up

A. Give a brief oral or written report. Tell about the worst or best teacher you ever had. In your report, consider including some of the following details:

What was your teacher's name?

What subject did this person teach?

At what school?

Where was the school located?

How long ago did you have this teacher?

What made this teacher so wonderful or so terrible? Give an example to show this.

How did this teacher affect your attitude toward school?

How did this teacher affect your attitude toward teachers?

B. *From the list of subjects commonly taught in secondary schools, choose the six subjects that you would most like to study. If you are not sure what these subjects are, look them up in the dictionary. Compare your choices with your classmates' choices.*

algebra	art	biology
calculus	chemistry	drama
driver education	English	French
German	geometry	health
history	journalism	music
physical education	physics	psychology
Spanish	trigonometry	word processing

Your Choices

1. _____

2. _____

3. _____

4. _____

5. _____

6. _____

U N I T 17

The Changing Role of Women

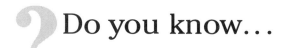 ## Do you know...

1. In what ways has the role of women been changing over the past twenty or thirty years?

2. When a man and a woman go out on a date, who usually pays?

Who Pays the Check?

Read the story.

I am Jennifer. In my senior year in high school, there were many exciting activities like dances, homecoming picnics, sports contests against the teachers, and, of course, the prom!

Prom night was coming, and tickets went on sale. They cost $89 for a couple. Single guys roamed the school, looking for girls to ask out. A friend told me that one of his friends wanted to go to the prom with me. Eventually I met the friend, Eddie, and we got along just fine. Gentleman-like, Eddie offered to pay for our prom tickets. However, he insisted that I pay for the prom pictures, and trying to do my part, I agreed. At the prom, everything went just great. We danced, ate, and chatted for at least five hours.

After the prom, we went to a restaurant and had dinner. The dinner was great, too, but when it was over, the trouble began. Eddie just sat there, even though he had finished eating. Thinking that he was tired, I just sat there too. Then it turned out that Eddie expected me to pay for the meal. I was horrified because, according to Chinese customs, a guy always pays for everything when he asks a girl out. I was already surprised when Eddie had insisted that I pay for the prom pictures, but this was too much for me. Eventually I paid and Eddie drove me home. I did not talk to him for a very long time. Later on, I found out that there is an American custom of "splitting the bill," where each individual pays half. It took me a long time to adapt to this custom!

homecoming—A school celebration welcoming back former students

prom—A formal school dance for students who are about to graduate

roamed—Wandered

chatted—Talked in a friendly, informal manner

adapt—Change to fit into a new situation

UNIT 17   *The Changing Role of Women*

Comprehension

A. *Tell whether these sentences are true or false.*

1. Prom tickets cost $89 for a couple.

2. Jennifer and Eddie were friends from class.

3. Eddie wanted Jennifer to pay for the prom tickets.

4. Eddie wanted Jennifer to pay for the dinner.

5. Jennifer had a great time at the prom.

6. Sharing costs on a date is both a Chinese custom and an American custom.

7. Jennifer is now used to the custom of splitting the bill with a boy.

B. *Answer these questions.*

1. What were some of the senior-year activities at Jennifer's high school?

2. How did Jennifer meet Eddie?

3. What was the first thing that surprised Jennifer?

4. Why did Eddie just sit when the meal was over?

5. Why was Jennifer surprised that she had to pay for the food?

6. How did Jennifer treat Eddie after that night?

C. *Give your opinion.*

1. Do you think it was fair for Eddie to want Jennifer to pay for the pictures? Why or why not?

2. How could the situation at the restaurant have been avoided?

3. Do you think Jennifer should have been so angry with Eddie? Explain.

4. Do you like the American custom of splitting expenses on dates? Explain your answer.

5. Do you think it is reasonable to expect high school students to spend so much money for prom activities?

CULTURE CAPSULE

Women's roles have been changing. Thirty years ago most married women were housewives and did not work outside the home. Today, most women have jobs, including jobs—like truck drivers or business executives—that used to be held only by men.

With the changes in roles have come changes in customs. Women used to expect that men would open doors for them, but now they open their own. When a man invited a woman out for dinner, he was expected to pay for everything. Today, a woman might share the expenses when she goes out with a man. She can be the one who calls him up and asks him out. She might even pay the expenses for the entire date.

Cultural Exchange

A. Fill in the chart and then share your answers with your classmates.

Concerning Males and Females . . .	Your Country	United States
Do sons and daughters have the same household chores?		
Do sons and daughters receive the same amount of education?		
Are sons and daughters equally valued?		
After marriage, are daughters closer to their husband's family than their own family?		
Can women invite men out on dates?		
Can women pay when going out with men?		
Is it acceptable for women not to marry?		
Do married women with children work outside the home?		
In a divorce, who generally gets custody of the children?		

B. *Discuss these questions with your classmates.*

1. Are single mothers (those divorced or never married) approved or disapproved of in your culture? From your observation are they approved or disapproved of in American culture?

2. In your culture, are husbands looked down upon if their wives work outside the home?

3. In your culture, is it acceptable for a woman to be out alone at night? How does this compare with American culture?

4. What are the usual kinds of jobs that women have in your country? Would men ever have these jobs?

5. Are there any jobs held by women in the United States that would not be allowed in your country? Are there any jobs held by women in your country that you've never seen in the United States?

6. Do you think that the changing role of women has had a positive or a negative effect on American culture? Explain.

Expansion

Divide into groups of six to eight people. Each group chooses one of the issues listed below. Half of each group should make a list of reasons why they agree with the statement, and the other half should make a list of reasons why they disagree with the statement. Have both sides present their reasons to the rest of the class. The class can vote to see whether they agree or disagree. You can add other issues if you like.

1. It is time to elect a woman president of the United States.

2. Women should be able to become fighter pilots.

3. Girls should be allowed to play high school football.

4. Husbands should equally share housework and child-care responsibilities with their wives.

5. Married women should stay home and take care of their children.

6. If boys want to play with dolls they should be allowed to do so.

7. Single women should invite men out on dates.

8. Single women should share dating expenses with men.

Role Play

Work in pairs. Choose one of the following situations and role-play it for your classmates. Before you role-play, write the conversation.

Situation 1: Role-play "Who Pays the Check?" on page 128. Begin your role play at the table when Eddie just sits there waiting for Jennifer to pay the check.

Use these questions to help you write the conversation:

☐ Is Jennifer confused or surprised? Is she angry?

☐ Is Eddie confused or surprised? Is he angry?

Student A=Jennifer
Student B=Eddie

After you role-play, discuss these questions with your classmates:

☐ Does Jennifer remain angry with Eddie? Will she only want to date Chinese boys in the future?

☐ Does Eddie understand there was a problem of cultural differences?

☐ Will Eddie ever ask Jennifer out on a date again?

Situation 2: Mr. and Mrs. Berk both work and have small sons. One night after she picks up the boys from child care she goes home and starts dinner. When her husband gets home she asks him to fold the laundry. He replies, "That's not my job." Finish the story.

Use these questions to help you write the conversation:

☐ Does Mrs. Berk get angry? How can she convince Mr. Berk that it *is* his job?

☐ Does Mrs. Berk feel guilty asking Mr. Berk to do "women's work"?

☐ Does Mr. Berk get angry with his wife or is he just teasing her?

☐ Would Mr. Berk be willing to cook instead? Does he feel guilty for not agreeing to help?

> Student A=Mrs. Berk
> Student B=Mr. Berk

After you role-play, discuss these questions with your classmates:

☐ Does Mrs. Berk forgive Mr. Berk or does she stay angry?

☐ Is Mr. Berk angry with his wife or sympathetic?

☐ Does Mr. Berk regret what he said?

Follow-Up

A. *Give a brief oral or written report. Choose number 1 or 2.*

1. How would your life be different if you had been born the opposite sex?

2. When you were growing up, did your parents treat sons and daughters differently? If so, how?

If you choose number 1, consider including some of the following details:

> How would your parents have treated you differently?
>
> How would your education be different? Give an example.
>
> How would your work be different?
>
> How would your financial situation be different?
>
> Would you have more influence or power? less influence or power?
>
> How would your romantic life be different?
>
> How would your friendships be different?
>
> Would your life be a happier one if you had been born the opposite sex? Explain.

If you choose number 2, consider including some of the following details:

How were the household chores the same or different?

How were the educational expectations the same or different?

Could sons and daughters stay out until the same hours?

Could daughters go out alone unattended? Could sons?

When you have your own sons and daughters will you treat them the same way your parents did? Why or why not?

Now that you have your own sons and daughters have you raised them the same way your parents did? Why or why not?

B. *Make two lists. For one list write down all the advantages in being female. For the other list write down all the advantages in being male. Which list is longer? What does this tell you? Compare your lists with those of your classmates.*

UNIT 18

Attitudes Toward Aging

 ## Do you know...

1. Do many Americans look forward to growing older? Why or why not?

2. What are some disadvantages of growing older?

Jack's Tale

Read the story.

When my family emigrated from a small village in Canton, China, we brought not only our luggage, but also our village's rules, customs, and superstitions. One of the rules is that youngsters should always respect elders. Unfortunately, this rule resulted in my very first embarrassment in the United States.

I had a part-time job as a waiter in a Chinese restaurant. One time, when I was serving food to a middle-aged couple, the wife asked me how the food could be served so quickly. I told her that I had made sure they got their food quickly because I always respect the elderly. As soon as I said that, her face showed great displeasure. My manager, who had overheard, took me aside and gave me a long lecture about how sensitive Americans are and how they dislike the description "old." I then walked back to the table and apologized to the wife. After the couple listened to my explanation, they understood that the incident was caused by cultural differences, so they laughed and were no longer angry.

In my village in China, people are proud of being older. Not that many people survive to the age of fifty or sixty, and people who reach such an age have the most knowledge and experience. Youngsters always respect older people because they know they can learn from this valuable experience.

However, in the United States aging is considered a problem since "old" means that a person is going to retire or that the body is not functioning so well. Here many people try to avoid old age by doing exercises or jogging, and women put on makeup hoping to look young. When I told the couple in the restaurant that I respect the elderly, they got angry because this made them feel they had failed to retain their youth. I had told them something they didn't want to hear.

As a result of this experience, I have changed the way I am with older people. This does not mean that I don't respect them anymore; I still respect them, but now I don't express my feelings through words.

superstitions—Beliefs that are not based on reason but are based on magic or old ideas

---

UNIT 18 *Attitudes Toward Aging*

Comprehension

A. *Tell whether these sentences are true or false.*

1. When Jack came to America he only brought his luggage.

2. Jack brought the couple their food very fast because he wanted a good tip.

3. When Jack called the couple "elderly," they were displeased.

4. Jack's manager wanted to fire him.

5. After Jack apologized, the couple left the restaurant angry.

6. Jack respects older people because they have the most knowledge and experience.

7. Jack no longer respects the elderly.

B. *Answer these questions.*

1. What is one of the rules that Jack brought with him from China?

2. What did Jack do that offended the couple?

3. What did Jack's manager explain to Jack?

4. How did the couple respond after Jack apologized?

5. According to Jack, why was the couple upset?

6. As a result of this experience how has Jack changed?

C. *Give your opinion.*

1. Do you think Jack's boss handled the situation well? Explain.

2. Do you think Jack handled the situation well after he apologized? Explain.

3. Do you think the couple handled the situation well after Jack apologized? Explain. What other reaction might they have had?

4. Do you think Jack made the right decision not to express his feelings through words anymore? Why or why not?

5. What is your opinion of Jack?

CULTURE CAPSULE

America tends to be a youth-oriented culture. Although some cultures value getting old, in America people tend to value being young. This is shown, for example, by the large amounts of money spent on products that prevent wrinkles or cover up gray hair. Being a "senior citizen" (sixty-five years of age or older) brings certain privileges, like reduced prices for theater and travel tickets. But because of society's attitudes, many people probably do not look forward to growing old. However, attitudes toward aging might be changing. In a sense, the American population is aging; by the year 2030, over 20 percent of Americans will be sixty-five years or older. As the population ages, Americans are becoming more aware that older people have a lot to contribute to society.

tends to—Likely to behave in a certain way

youth-oriented—Believing in being and staying young

wrinkles—Creases and lines on the skin, especially the face

privileges—Special rights or advantages given to an individual or group

Cultural Exchange

A. *Fill in the chart and then share your answers with your classmates.*

When It Comes to Aging . . .	Your Country	United States
Is it acceptable to ask people their age?		
At what age do people retire?		
At what age are people considered old?		
Do people try to slow the effects of aging? If so, how? (hair dye? surgery? other?)		
What are the privileges of aging? (discounted prices? respect? other?)		

B. *Discuss these questions with your classmates.*

1. In your culture, do you celebrate birthdays? Which birthdays are the special ones?

2. In your culture, where do the elderly live and with whom?

3. In your culture, does one particular child take care of elderly parents or do all the children share the responsibility? Explain.

4. In your culture, are elderly men treated the same as elderly women? Explain.

5. In the United States, do you have much contact with people of different ages, including older people? Do you think that in your own country you would have more or less contact with older people? Explain your answer.

6. What have you observed about attitudes toward the elderly and toward aging in America? How are these attitudes similar to attitudes in your culture? How are they different?

7. What do you see as advantages of getting old in the United States as opposed to in your country? What do you see as disadvantages?

Expansion

Conduct a survey on attitudes about aging. With a partner, ask and answer the following questions. Then compare answers with your classmates. You may also want to ask people outside of the classroom for their opinions.

1. Do you think there is a certain age at which you will be old? If so, about what age?

2. When you are old would you consider:

    a. lying about your age?

    b. changing your gray hair to another color?

    c. using cosmetics to make you seem younger?

    d. having surgery to make your face look younger?

    e. wearing clothes made for younger people?

3. What kinds of things do you look forward to doing when you get old?

4. Do you consider older people more valuable than younger people, younger people more valuable than older people, or both equally valuable? Explain.

# Role Play

Work in groups of three. Choose one of the following situations and role-play it for your classmates. Before you role-play, write the conversation.

> **Situation 1:** Role-play "Jack's Tale" on page 136. Begin your role play when Jack brings the couple their food.

Use these questions to help you write the conversation:

- ☐ Is the lady angry, hurt, or shocked by what Jack tells her?
- ☐ Does she say anything to Jack?
- ☐ Is the manager angry? Is he worried about losing these customers? Is he sympathetic toward the customers? Is he understanding of Jack's ignorance of American ways?
- ☐ Does Jack feel guilty or embarrassed when the manager talks to him? Does he worry about losing his job? What does he now say to the lady?

> Student A=Jack
> Student B=the lady
> Student C=the manager

After you role-play, discuss these questions with your classmates:

- ☐ As a result of the experience, did Jack feel embarrassed or was he relieved?
- ☐ Do you think Jack handled the situation well?
- ☐ In the end, was the lady sympathetic toward Jack? Or was she still a little angry?

> **Situation 2:** Two people apply for the same job. One person is young and attractive and has almost no experience. The other is in his or her sixties and has had a lot of experience. The interviewer speaks to them both and must decide who to hire. Write the ending.

Use these questions to help you write the conversation:

☐ What work is involved? How much experience is needed?
What kind of employee is the interviewer looking for?
What are the interviewer's attitudes toward older people?

☐ How does the younger person try to convince the interviewer that his or her lack of experience does not matter?

☐ Is the older person worried that the interviewer just wants to hire someone young? How does this individual try to impress the interviewer?

> Student A=the younger person
> Student B=the older person
> Student C=the interviewer

After you role-play, discuss these questions with your classmates:

☐ Why did the interviewer make the decision that was made?

☐ How did the younger person try to convince the interviewer?

☐ How did the older person try to convince the interviewer?

☐ Do you agree with the decision the interviewer made? Why or why not? Who would you have hired?

Follow-Up

A. *Give a brief oral or written report. Tell about an older person in your life who has influenced you. In your report, consider including some of the following details:*

Who is (was) the person?

What is (was) your relationship to this person?

Where does (did) this person live?

What does (did) this person look like?

How did you meet this person?

What makes this person so special? Give an example.

How has this person affected your life?

B. *Television report. Watch thirty to sixty minutes of TV and take notes about the older people you see in the commercials and in the shows. How are older people depicted? Some possible descriptions are given below. Add any others you can think of.*

Are They . . . ?

helpful	important	wise
leaders	insignificant	weak
stupid	grouchy	sweet

stars or minor characters

problems or problem solvers

Bring your report to class and compare it with your classmates' reports. After hearing all the reports, is there anything you can conclude about how older people are depicted?

UNIT 19

Stereotypes and Prejudice

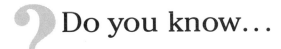

Do you know...

1. What is prejudice? Is prejudice common in the United States?

2. What can be done to fight prejudice?

Sticks and Stones

Read the story.

My name is Teresa. My parents are from Mexico but moved to the United States, where I was born. When I was twelve years old I was bused from my neighborhood to a community nearby for junior high school. My reaction when I got to the school was one of culture shock. The majority of students, teachers, and staff were Anglo. I had never been in such an environment before. Up to then I had been in a completely Hispanic neighborhood and school. The first thing that ran through my head was, where have I been?

I felt as if I was in another world of people who looked different, acted different, spoke and dressed differently. I didn't know how to behave or what to say. They wore what I later discovered to be designer jeans and backpacks. They also seemed to be wealthy, because they paid cash for their meals while I used reduced meal tickets.

I didn't have any friends at first. I didn't know any of the students who rode the bus with me, and in most of my classes I was the only Hispanic. I was shy and embarrassed. I felt very intimidated by all these very verbal and confident individuals. I also felt vibrations of hate and resentment from these people, although I wasn't sure why. I had no one to talk to or turn to for help who I thought would be able to understand. I had no Hispanic role models.

During the first week of school, there was an incident. As my bus was leaving the school, a bunch of Anglo kids began throwing eggs at the bus and screaming, "Go home, beaners!" I had no idea what a "beaner" was or why the kids would be so cruel. This incident stayed with me. I earned A's in most of my classes. As time went on, I became friends with other Hispanics and with Anglo kids. But I still felt hurt, mad, and a little confused. Deep inside I knew that the majority of the Anglo kids did not want any "beaners" in their school. They must have felt invaded, and I

sticks and stones—The first words of a verse that parents teach children to say to other children who call them bad names: *Sticks and stones may break my bones, but names can never hurt me.*

(to be) bused—Sending children by bus from their own school to a generally better school

intimidated—Frightened, often caused by threats of violence

vibrations—Emotional sensations

role models—People to look up to and copy their achievements and behavior

cruel—Feeling pleasure in the pain or suffering of another person

invaded—Taken under control by outsiders

UNIT 19 *Stereotypes and Prejudice*

think that since they did not really know many Hispanics, they probably had hundreds of stereotypes about us.

How did I feel at the end of my first year? I felt that my experience had been very meaningful and educational. I was amazed by how much I had learned about another part of society. My attitudes toward these "other" people had changed greatly. Above all, I felt that my eyes had been opened to more of what life had to offer and that I had learned quite a lot academically, probably more than I would have learned if I had gone to junior high school in my neighborhood.

stereotypes—To think of a thing or a person as an example of a general type, generally negative

Comprehension

A. *Tell whether these sentences are true or false.*

1. Before junior high school, Teresa had never been in a school with Anglos.

2. Teresa's first reaction to her new school was culture shock.

3. Teresa made friends at the new school right away.

4. Teresa paid cash for her meals.

5. Some Anglo students called the Hispanic students "beaners."

6. Some Anglo students threw eggs at Teresa's bus.

7. Teresa did not get good grades at her new school.

8. At the end of the year, Teresa decided she would switch back to the junior high school in her neighborhood.

B. *Answer these questions.*

1. Why was Teresa shocked by her new school?

2. How did the students dress there?

3. What incident occurred during Teresa's first week of school?

4. How did this incident make Teresa feel?

5. Why does Teresa think the students acted that way?

6. Besides academic opportunities, what else did Teresa get out of being bused?

C. *Give your opinion.*

1. Why do you think the students threw eggs at the bus and called the Hispanic students names?

2. Do you agree with Teresa that even though she eventually became friends with the Anglo kids, deep inside they did not want Hispanics at their school? Why or why not?

3. Do you agree with Teresa that it is valuable to step outside one's own territory and see what other opportunities there are? Why or why not?

4. Do you think busing is a good way to achieve this?

CULTURE CAPSULE

The United States has often been called a "melting pot"—a place where people from many different countries blend together and all become Americans. But many people argue that this description is not accurate. They say the United States is more like a salad bowl—many ingredients are tossed together but never completely blend. On the one hand, this is what makes the United States more interesting: People are not just Americans; they are Americans and something else. On the other hand, the differences have sometimes led to problems—to stereotypes and prejudice, to discrimination, and at times even violence.

With the civil rights movement, led by African Americans in the 1950s and 1960s, some important changes were made to fight prejudice and discrimination. Busing, sending African American and Hispanic children from poor school districts to Anglo schools in better neighborhoods, was an attempt to provide equal educational opportunities. As American society becomes more racially and ethnically mixed, many more changes must be made.

blend—To mix together into a smooth and unified substance

tossed—Mixed lightly

prejudice—Unfair and often unfavorable feeling or opinion not based on reason or enough knowledge

discrimination—Unfair treatment

civil rights movement—Organized actions to obtain equal rights, privileges, and protection for minorities

Cultural Exchange

Discuss these questions with your classmates.

1. In your country, are there any ethnic, racial, or religious groups that faced prejudice and discrimination in the past? Do any continue to face prejudice and discrimination today? Explain.

2. Are there any other groups in your culture that you think face some prejudice and discrimination? For example, are physically disabled people discriminated against? People who are divorced? Single mothers? Explain.

3. In your culture, are there any kinds of government policies or laws to discourage discrimination?

4. In your culture, do people of different ethnic groups usually socialize with one another? Explain.

5. In your culture, do people object to marriages between persons of different ethnic groups, races, or religions? Explain.

6. In your country, do people from different groups live in different neighborhoods?

7. Have you seen people in the United States discriminate against others? Have you ever felt discriminated against in the United States?

8. Do you think the amount of prejudice in the United States is increasing or decreasing? What do you think can be done to fight stereotypes and prejudice?

Expansion

Work in groups. Choose one of the situations. In each of the situations someone faces a problem. In your group, discuss the three possible solutions listed below and the consequences of the solutions. Choose one of the solutions and compare your group's decision with other groups.

1. Mike is a very successful sales representative and an outstanding employee. He has recently begun playing with a rock band after work and has let his hair grow to shoulder length. Mike's company wants him to cut his hair. They say it is bad for the company image for him to look that way. Mike says that as long as he is doing his job well, which he is, the company has no right to tell him how to wear his hair, but the company threatens to fire him unless he cuts it.

   Mike says that the company is discriminating against him. What do you think?

   Our group has decided that:

   a. Mike should quit and find another company that will accept his hair length.

   b. Mike should cut his hair and stay with the company.

   c. Mike should take legal action against his company so that he can keep his hair as long as he wants and still continue working there.

2. A corporation has asked its office manager, Leila, to move and set up a new department of the company in a city some 2,000 miles away. In exchange, the company promises to promote Leila to a higher position. Leila moves her family, successfully opens up the department, has it running smoothly, and the company praises Leila for her accomplishment. However, when the time comes for Leila's promotion, the company backs down and puts a male employee into the higher position instead.

Leila claims that the company is discriminating against her because she is a woman. What do you think?

Our group has decided that:

a. Leila should quit and find another job.

b. Leila should accept the company's decision.

c. Leila should take legal action against the company.

Role Play

Work in pairs. Choose one of the following situations and role-play it for your classmates. Before you role-play, write the conversation.

Situation 1: Role-play "Sticks and Stones" on pages 144 and 145. Begin your role play at school with a classmate calling Teresa names and throwing an egg at Teresa's bus. Have Teresa confront the classmate. Write the ending.

Use these questions to help you write the conversation:

☐ Is Teresa angry, afraid, or is she shocked?

☐ Is the classmate mean or ignorant? Does the classmate feel guilty when Teresa confronts him or her?

> Student A=Teresa
> Student B=the classmate

After you role-play, discuss these questions with your classmates:

☐ Did Teresa feel better after she confronted the classmate or did she feel more angry?

☐ Did the classmate feel sorry afterwards?

☐ What do you think of the ending? Is there any chance that Teresa and the classmate will become friends?

Situation 2: Bill Gillis is twenty-four years old. He has fallen madly in love and wants to marry Sara, who is ten years older than he is. Sara also has two teenage children from her former marriage. When Bill tells his mother about his marriage plans she becomes very angry. She is strongly opposed to this marriage. They have an argument about it. How does the argument end?

Use these questions to help you write the conversation:

☐ What are Mrs. Gillis's objections to this marriage? What kind of stereotypes do you think she has about divorced women? Does she object because Sara is too old for her son or does she mostly object to the children? What reasons can she give without sounding too prejudiced?

☐ Is Bill shocked that his mother is against the marriage even before meeting Sara? Is he surprised that his mother is against his marrying an "older woman"? How can he convince her that there is no real reason to object if he and Sara love one another? Will he feel guilty if he goes against his mother's wishes?

Student A=Bill
Student B=Mrs. Gillis

After you role-play, discuss these questions with your classmates:

☐ Did Mrs. Gillis give a convincing and reasonable argument for her son not to marry Sara? If she succeeded, will Bill be resentful? How will this affect their future relationship?

☐ If Bill convinced his mother, will his relationship with her be negatively affected? What kind of relationship can he expect between his mother and his wife? How will the children be affected?

☐ In American culture, why do you think it is more acceptable for a woman to marry an older man than for a man to marry an older woman? What kind of prejudice exists about marrying someone who has been married before—especially someone who has children?

Follow-Up

A. Give a brief oral or written report. Choose number 1 or 2.

1. Tell about a time when you were the victim of prejudice because of religion, culture, race, sex, age, physical disability, or because you couldn't speak English very well.

2. Tell about a time when you felt prejudiced against someone else because of that person's religion, culture, race, sex, age, or physical disability.

In your report, consider including some of the following details:

How long ago did this happen?

Where were you living at the time?

Who were the persons involved?

What happened?

How did you react?

How did others react?

What was the immediate effect of this experience?

What have you learned from this experience?

B. *With a partner, use an encyclopedia to research Native Americans, a group that has suffered a lot from prejudice and discrimination, so much so that today most live in isolated, poor conditions on land called "reservations."*

1. Choose a Native American tribe from the list below, or choose another tribe, and write down information about it.

2. Tell where the tribe is located, give some information about its culture (e.g., clothing, housing, language, customs, arts and crafts), and if you can, find out how the tribe has changed over the years as a result of contact with other Americans.

3. Share the information with your classmates.

Apache	Klamath	Seminole
Arapaho	Mohican	Shoshone
Blackfoot	Navaho	Sioux
Chickasaw	Nez Percé	Tlingit
Iroquois	Pawnee	Winnebago
Kiowa	Pueblo	

Religious Practices and Beliefs

Do you know...

1. What are some of the religions that are practiced in the United States?

2. Have you discovered any religious practices that have surprised you?

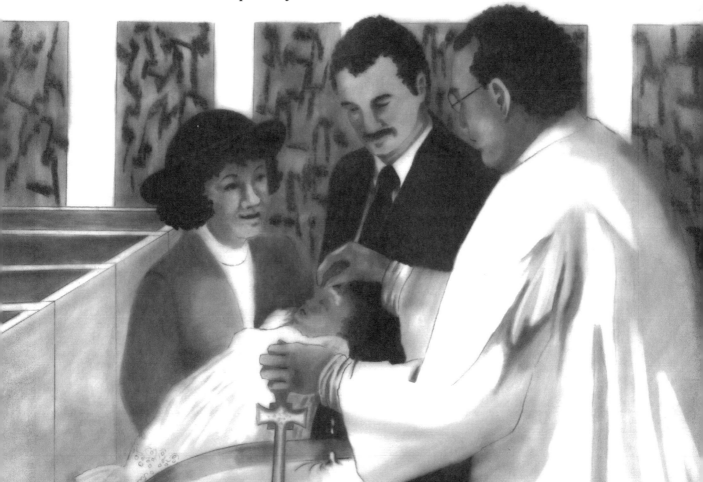

The Surprise

Read the story.

I came from Mexico, and my name is Amalia. Like most people, my family came to the United States for better opportunities in employment and education. Learning a new language wasn't easy, and what was even more difficult was learning to live with people from different cultures—not just the American culture, but many other cultures too. One of the embarrassing experiences I have had involved my best friend Silvia, who is from Venezuela and is a Jehovah's Witness.

When Silvia told me she was a Jehovah's Witness, I didn't know what that meant. She explained it was a religion. On her sixteenth birthday, Silvia invited me to her house. I was really excited. I thought there would be a party, so the day before I bought Silvia a present. It was an antique music box. When my dad dropped me off at her house I was surprised because the house seemed lonely and silent. I knocked at the door, and her mom answered. She greeted me with a kiss on the cheek and a hug. Then she invited me in. As I entered the living room, I saw a group of people. I greeted them and sat down. A few seconds later, Silvia came downstairs. As she greeted me with a hug and a kiss, I took out the present and said, "Happy Birthday!"

All of a sudden the people in the room stopped talking and stared at Silvia and me. I looked at Silvia with a puzzled look. She was just looking down at the ground with a face as red as a tomato. After a few minutes of silence, she said, "I'm sorry, but I can't accept your present. It was really sweet of you." I froze. I was embarrassed, hurt, and humiliated. Tears rolled down my cheeks. I didn't know what to do. Here I was in the middle of the room with all those people looking at me and not saying anything. I wished they would at least laugh at me or something.

After a few minutes I came to reality and ran out of the room. I ran all the way to the driveway. Silvia came running after me. Then she explained that in her religion, they did not celebrate birthdays or holidays

Jehovah's Witness—A Christian sect founded in the 1870s in Pennsylvania whose principles include that religious belief is most important

froze—Unable to move

humiliated—Lost the respect of others; felt humble

of any kind, and that the people in her living room were members of her congregation. She couldn't accept the present. It would have gotten her in trouble because it was like breaking the law. As I turned to look at her, I saw there were tears in her eyes. "So, I have to keep the present?" I asked. Sadly, she nodded yes, but she gave me a hug and I felt a little better.

As a result of this experience, I've learned not to make assumptions. Not everybody has the same tradition as I do. Now when I hear of a new religion I ask for information and make sure I don't have another misunderstanding.

congregation—those belonging to the same religious group

assumptions—things taken for granted without proof

Comprehension

A. *Tell whether these sentences are true or false.*

1. Amalia's family came to the United States for better job and education opportunities.

2. Silvia's family came from Mexico.

3. "Jehovah's Witness" refers to a kind of religion.

4. When Amalia got to Silvia's house she could tell the people there were having a party.

5. The other people in the house were members of Silvia's family.

6. Amalia cried when Silvia did not accept the present.

7. Amalia recovered and stayed for the evening.

B. *Answer these questions.*

1. What kind of present did Amalia buy for Silvia?

2. What happened when Amalia said "Happy Birthday" and gave her friend the present?

3. Why didn't Silvia accept the present?

4. How did Silvia feel about not accepting the present?

5. What did Amalia learn from this experience?

C. *Give your opinion.*

1. Do you think Silvia's mother should have tried to help Amalia understand? Why or why not?

2. Do you think Amalia should have run out of the house like she did? Why or why not?

3. Do you think that Silvia should have warned her friend in advance about Jehovah's Witnesses not celebrating birthdays? Why or why not?

4. Do you think that Amalia and Silvia will remain friends?

CULTURE CAPSULE

The United States has no official religion, as the U.S. Constitution says that church and state (religion and government) must be kept separate. This is not surprising since many early settlers (like many later immigrants) came to the United States for religious freedom. For this reason, it is also not so surprising that the United States has thousands of religions. Over 90 percent of Americans are Christians, but Christianity in the United States includes many different groups.

Religion plays an important part in the lives of many Americans. In addition to being places of worship, churches and temples are centers for education, social activities, and community events.

places of worship—Where one goes to pray or practice a religion

Cultural Exchange

Fill in the chart and then share your answers with your classmates. You may need to interview an American to help you complete it.

When It Comes to Religion . . .	Your Religion	Another Religion
Name of religion?		
Symbols? (cross? Star of David? crescent moon? other?)		
Leader's title? (priest? rabbi? minister? mullah? other?)		

When It Comes to Religion . . .	Your Religion	Another Religion
Where does the congregation gather? (church? mosque? temple? home? other?)		
Special fasting days? (name of celebration? date?)		
Special feast days? (name of celebration? date?)		
Ways to deal with sin? (confession? fasting? other?)		
Kinds of offerings? (flowers? money? other?)		
Rituals for babies? (naming? circumcision?) When done?		
Baptism? At what age? Takes place where?		
Rituals on reaching adulthood? At what age for boys? for girls? Name of ceremony?		
Rituals for dead? (burial? cremation?) When done? What happens?		
Memorial ceremonies on anniversaries of death? What happens?		
Special blessings for food? (wine? grapes? noodles? bread?)		

Expansion

See how many names of members of twenty different religions you can find hidden in the Word Search Game. Words can go up and down, forward and backward, and they may overlap.

```
M E N N O N I T E I D E N C R E K A U Q
A P V D E B K S U E F B H N U I L S N J
E I O T S A T I P H D K I A N C N E I O
W S G S H C T D C L M C G R L S I V T O
F C K I L E A O R H X N J E D F N E A L
H O B T J I Q H I N D U F H O J Y N R X
S P C P T C A T H O L I C T R E G T I O
I A O A B T M E O B A E B U D H I H A D
W L L B G N O M R P C V Q L Y O J D N O
E I G P R E S B Y T E R I A N V L A U H
J A C E E I L I S N Q H S I M A M Y Q T
P N Z N T M E H A P O O V R D H I A J R
F B P T G H M O R H C M E G P S H D F O
J I K E R E X E K I S G H Y I W B V G N
N A O C B C R W H T M B Q E F I G E O A
O H D O P M H O A Q F D Y Z M T N N H I
M A R S K C C A X F P K C Z E N J T H S
R B S T J Q A M G H V J A D L E B I K S
O M V A K F I N I Z Z A B D K S O S A U
M T D L B R A C D B U D D H I S T T R R
```

Amish	Jehovah's Witness	Pentecostal
Bahai	Jewish	Presbyterian
Baptist	Lutheran	Quaker
Buddhist	Mennonite	Russian Orthodox
Catholic	Methodist	Seventh-day Adventist
Episcopalian	Mormon	Unitarian
Hindu	Moslem	

 *Role Play*

Work in pairs. Choose one of the following situations and role-play it for your classmates. Before you role-play, write the conversation.

Situation 1: Role-play "The Surprise" on pages 152 and 153. Begin your role play when Amalia hands the present to Silvia and wishes her a "Happy Birthday." Follow the girls outside to the driveway.

Use these questions to help you write the conversation:

☐ Is Amalia more shocked or hurt?

☐ Is Silvia embarrassed because the other people are there?

☐ Does she feel sympathy for Amalia?

Student A=Amalia
Student B=Silvia

After the role play, discuss these questions with your classmates:

☐ At the end of the episode how did Amalia feel?

☐ How did Silvia feel?

☐ How do you think the girls' friendship was affected?

Situation 2: Donna invites her friend Abby to her grandmother's funeral. Donna and her family are very upset when Abby arrives dressed completely in white. In Donna's religion only dark colors are appropriate for a funeral. Abby cannot understand why people look at her so strangely at the funeral because in her religion one must wear white to funerals. Does Donna tell Abby what the problem is? Write the ending.

Continued on the following page

Use these questions to help you write the conversation:

☐ Is Abby shocked or embarrassed when she gets to the funeral?

☐ Is Donna shocked at seeing Abby in white or is she angry?

☐ Does she feel guilty for not having discussed this custom with Abby ahead of time?

Student A=Abby
Student B=Donna

After you role-play, discuss these questions with your classmates:

☐ Did Abby still feel close to Donna? Did she remain embarrassed?

☐ Did Donna forgive Abby? Has their friendship been damaged by this experience?

Follow-Up

A. *Give a brief oral or written report. Step by step, describe a ceremony that you enjoy from your own religion or a ceremony you have seen and enjoyed from another religion. When you do this be sure to use words like:*

> First (First the bells rang . . .)
>
> Next or Second (Next the parents brought in the baby . . .)
>
> After that (After that they threw rice . . .)
>
> Finally or Last of all (Finally they threw dirt on the grave . . .)

B. *On a piece of paper illustrate a religious ceremony you have seen and enjoyed. Compare your drawing with your classmates' drawings.*

ANSWER KEY

Page 5, Clothing

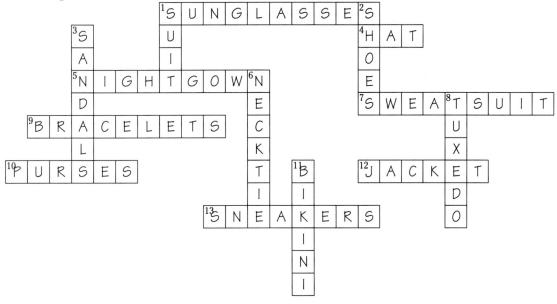

Page 20, Health and Illness

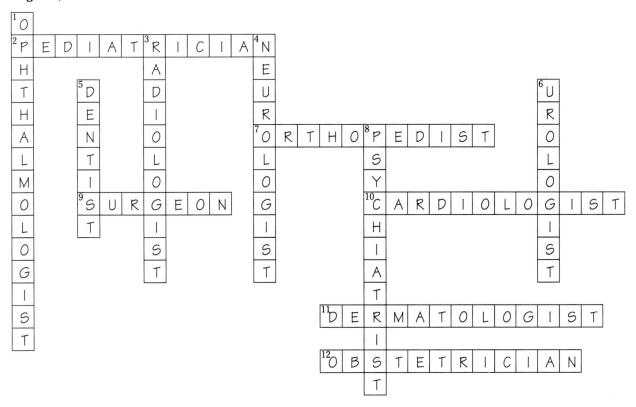

Page 99, Weddings

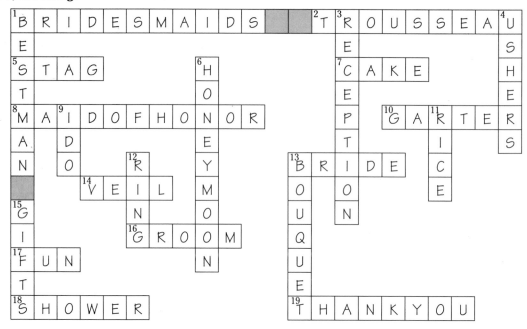

Page 156, Religious Practices and Beliefs

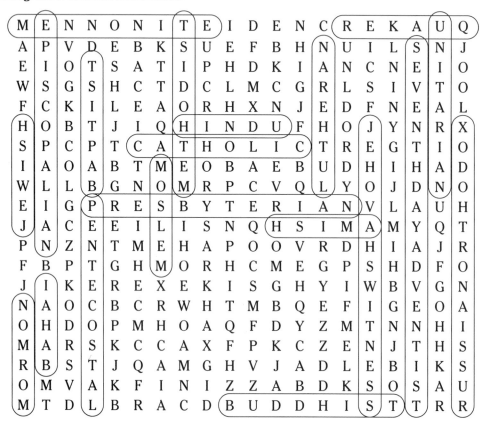